Draw CUTE ANIMALS For Kids

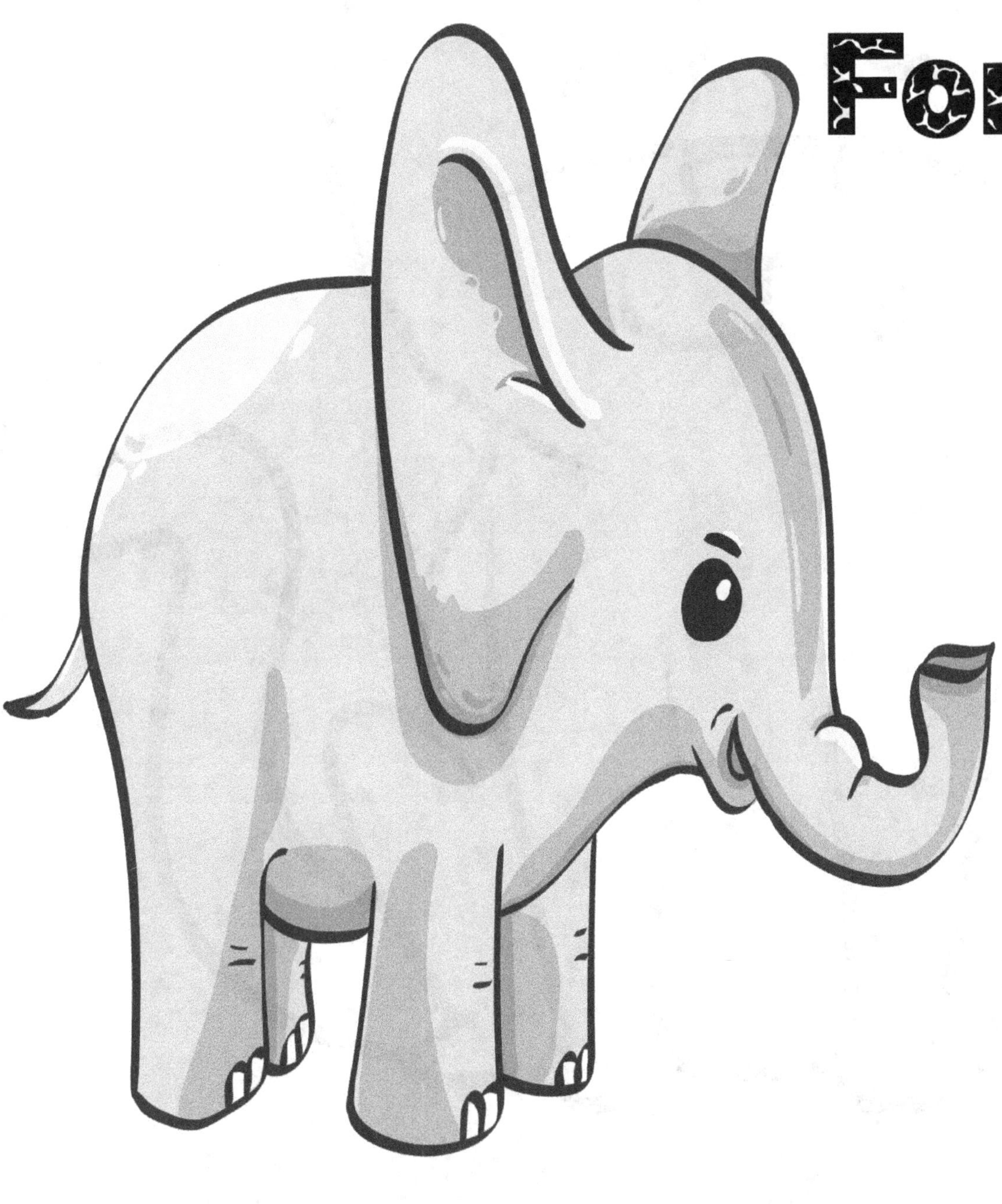

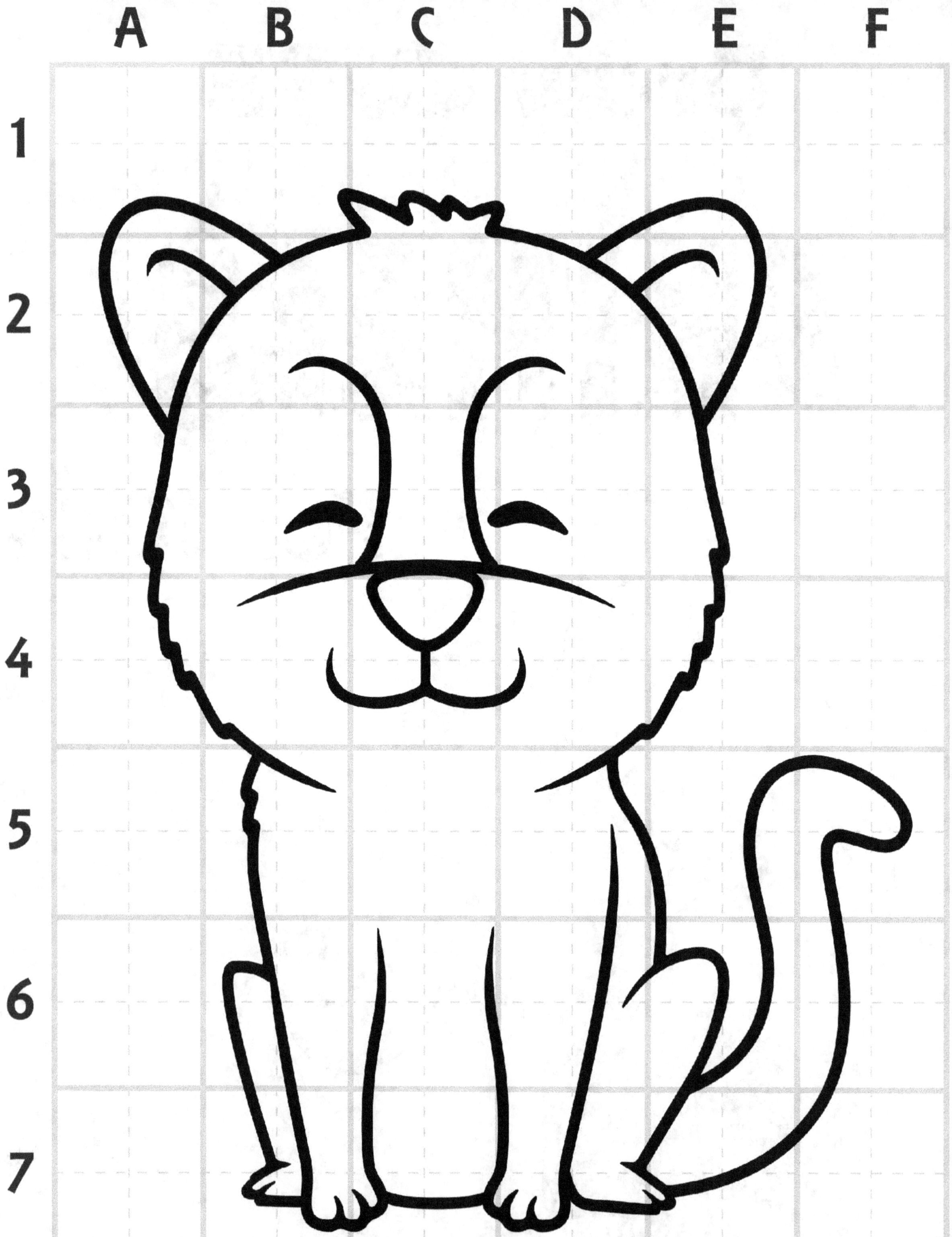
A
B
C
D
E
F
1
2
3
4
5
6
7

Your Drawing

	A	B	C	D	E	F
1						
2						
3						
4						
5						
6						
7						

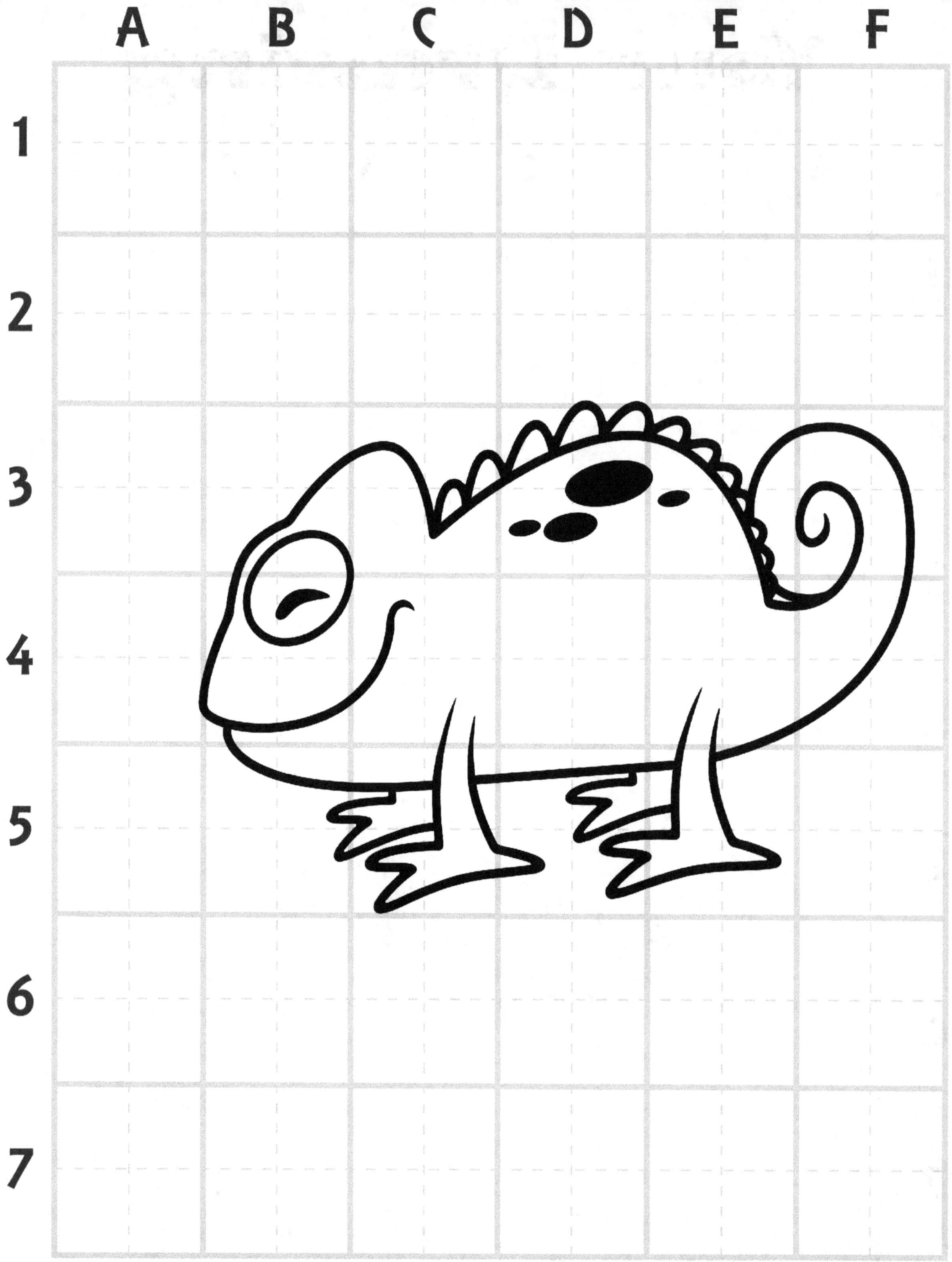
A
B
C
D
E
F
1
2
3
4
5
6
7

Your Drawing

	A	B	C	D	E	F
1						
2						
3						
4						
5						
6						
7						

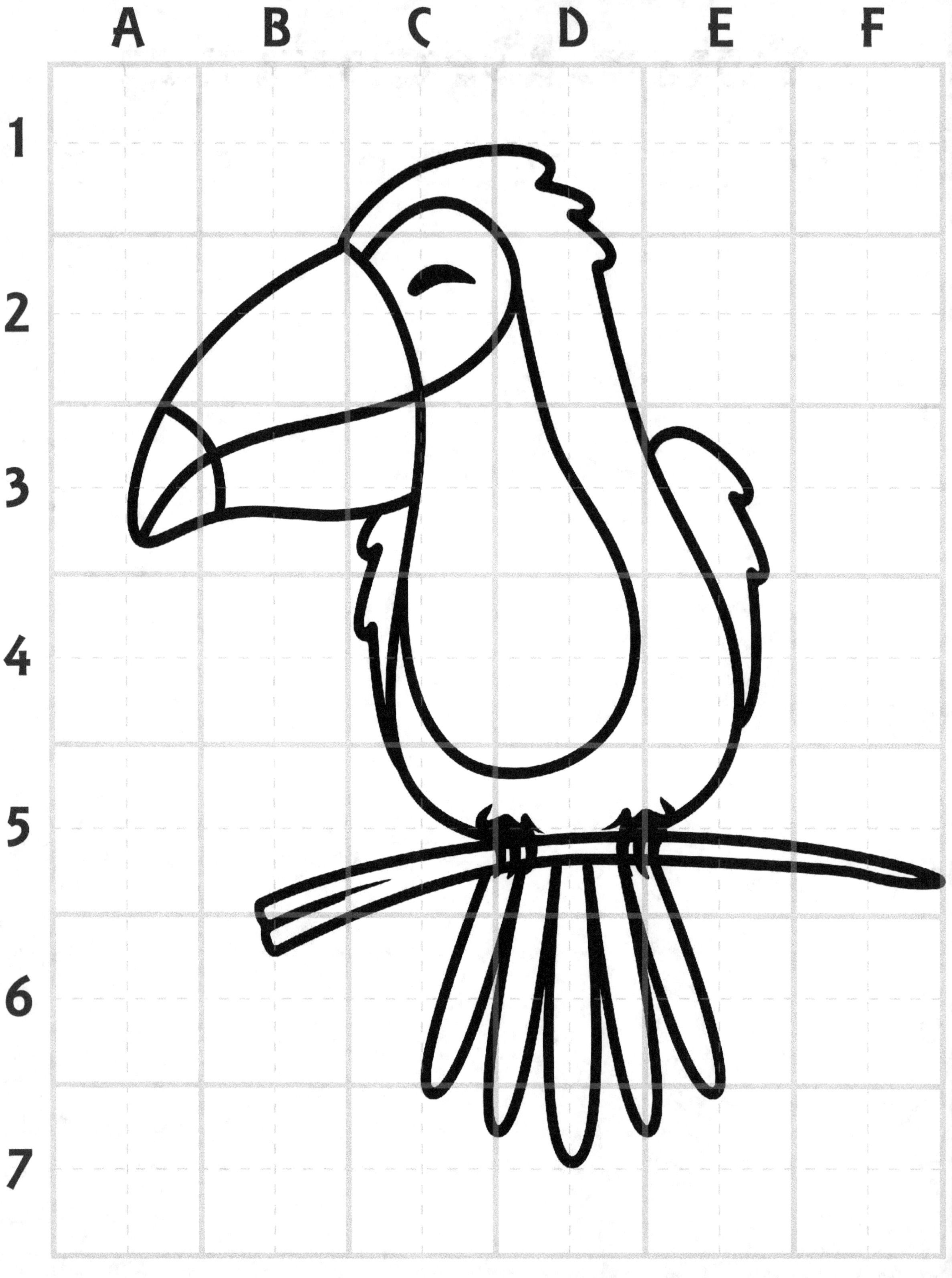
A B C D E F
1
2
3
4
5
6
7

Your Drawing

	A	B	C	D	E	F
1						
2						
3						
4						
5						
6						
7						

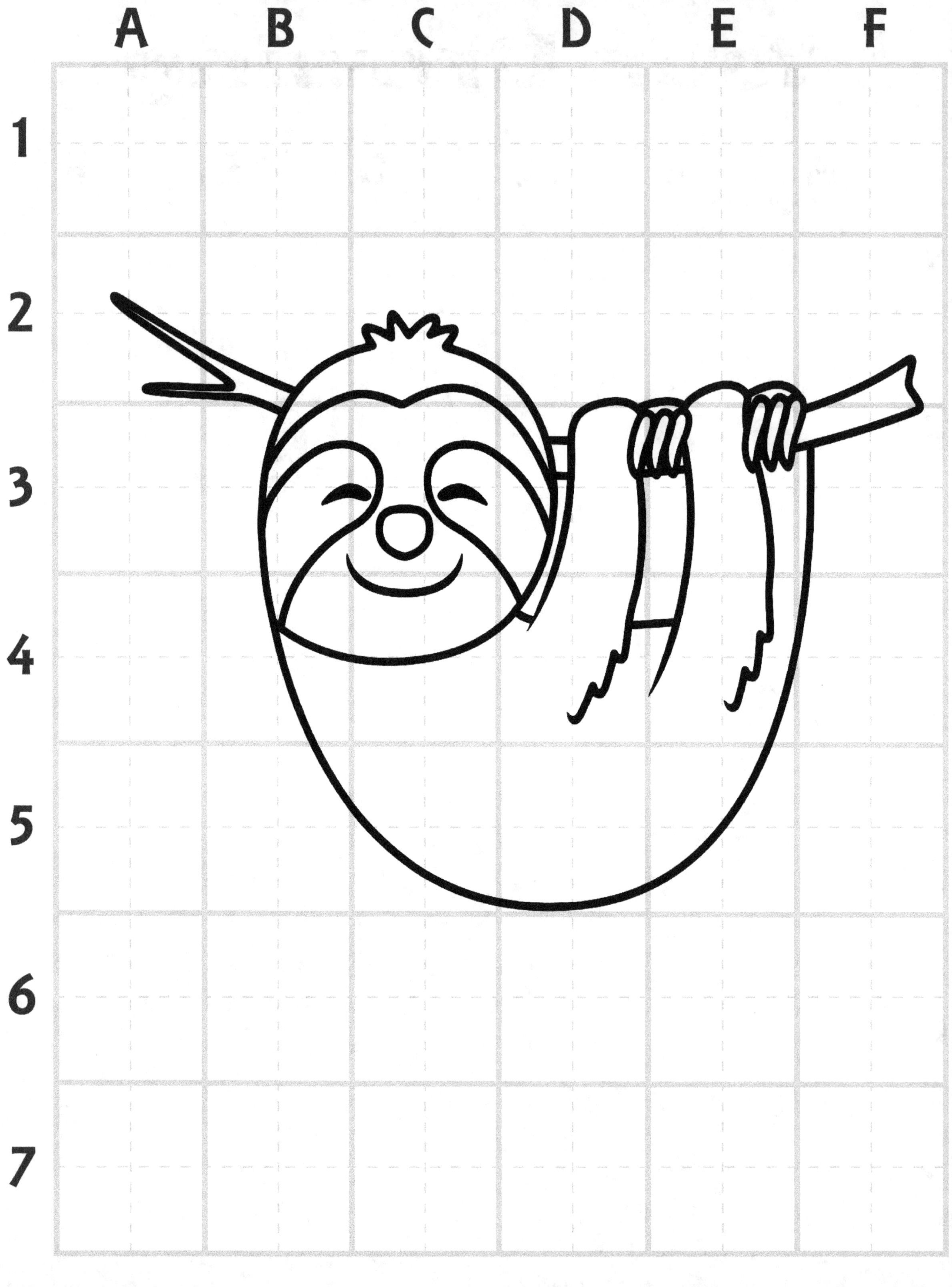
A B C D E F
1 2 3 4 5 6 7

Your Drawing

	A	B	C	D	E	F
1						
2						
3						
4						
5						
6						
7						

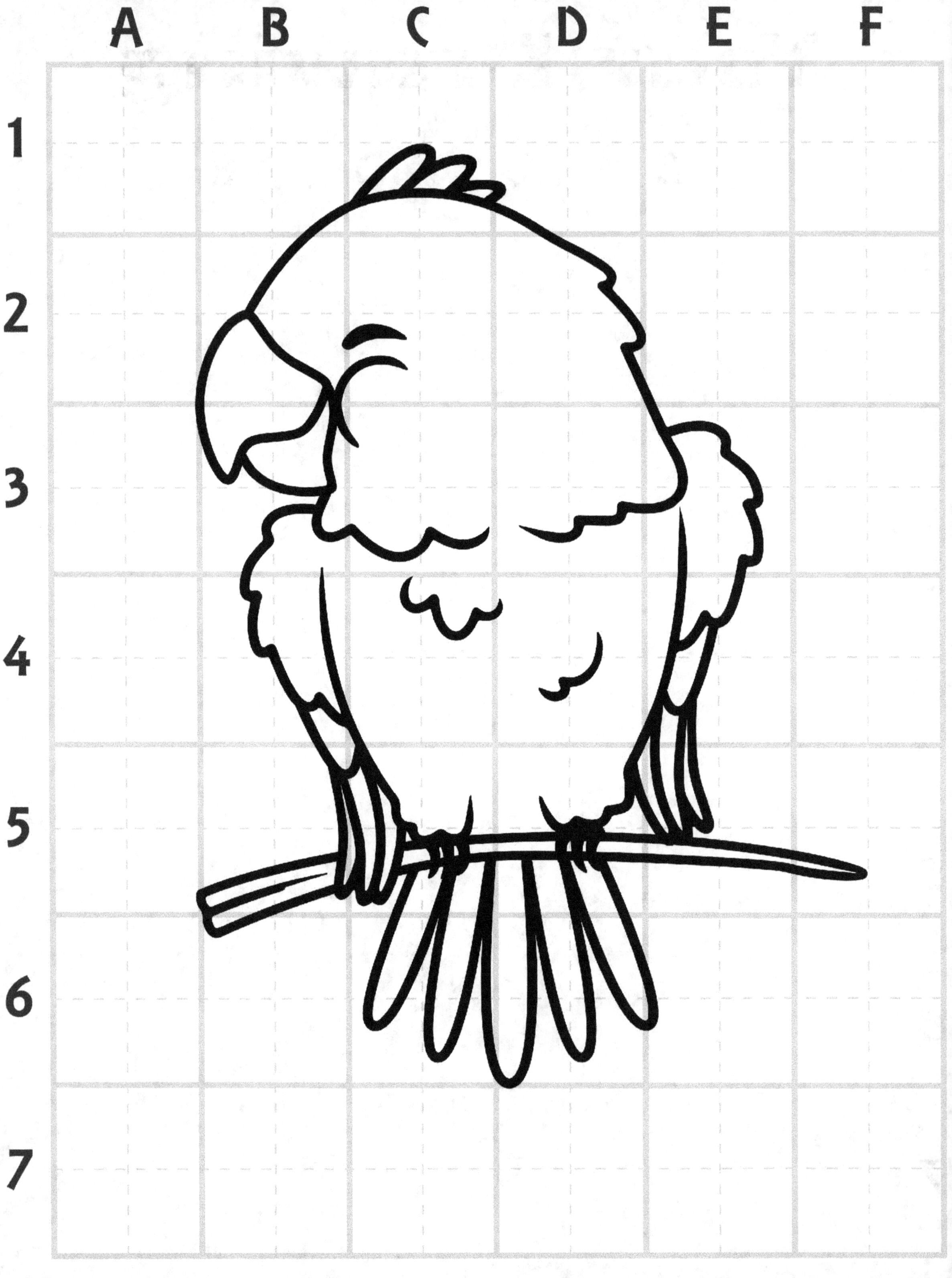
A B C D E F
1 2 3 4 5 6 7

Your Drawing

	A	B	C	D	E	F
1						
2						
3						
4						
5						
6						
7						

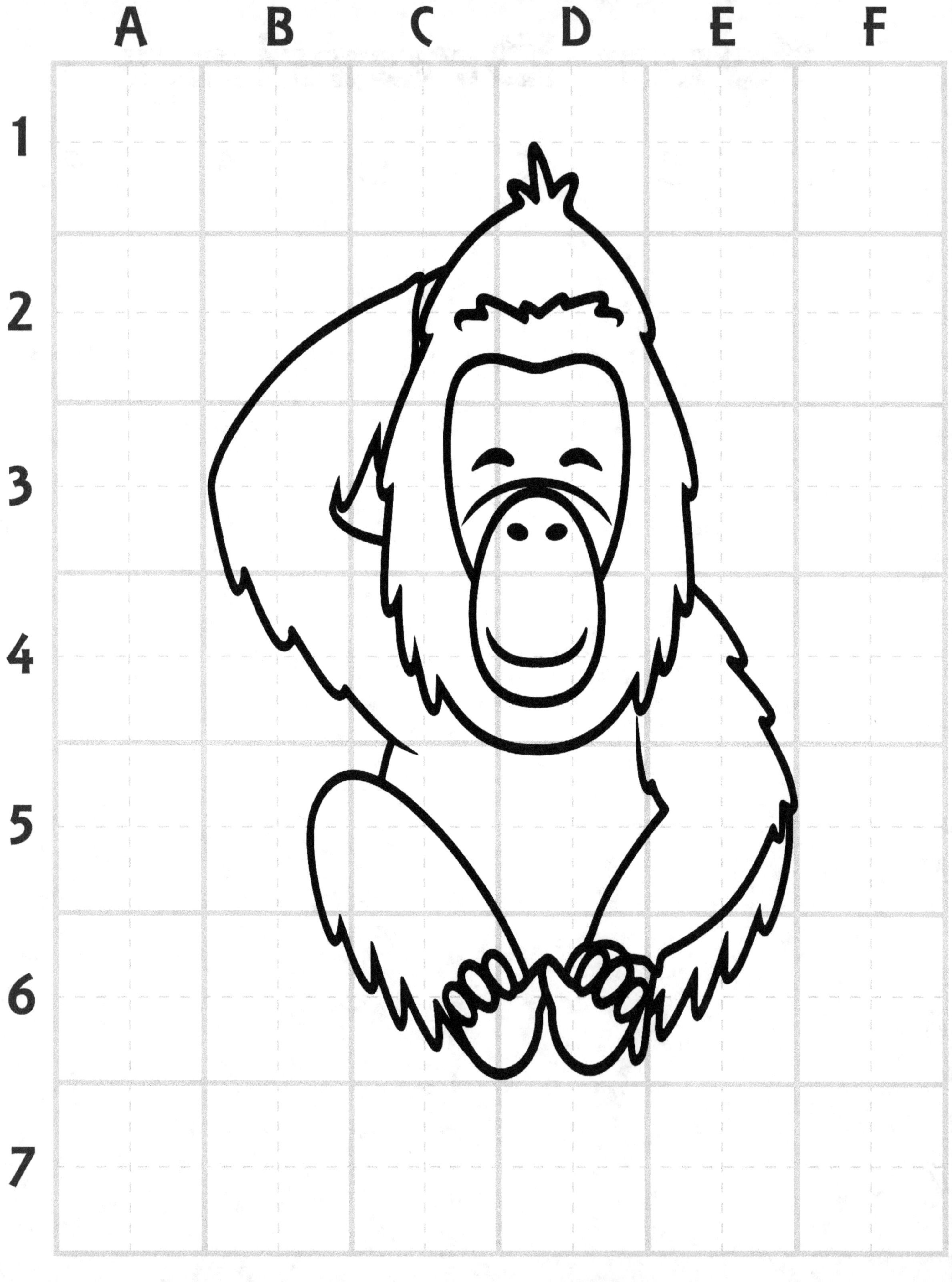
A
B
C
D
E
F
1
2
3
4
5
6
7

Your Drawing

	A	B	C	D	E	F
1						
2						
3						
4						
5						
6						
7						

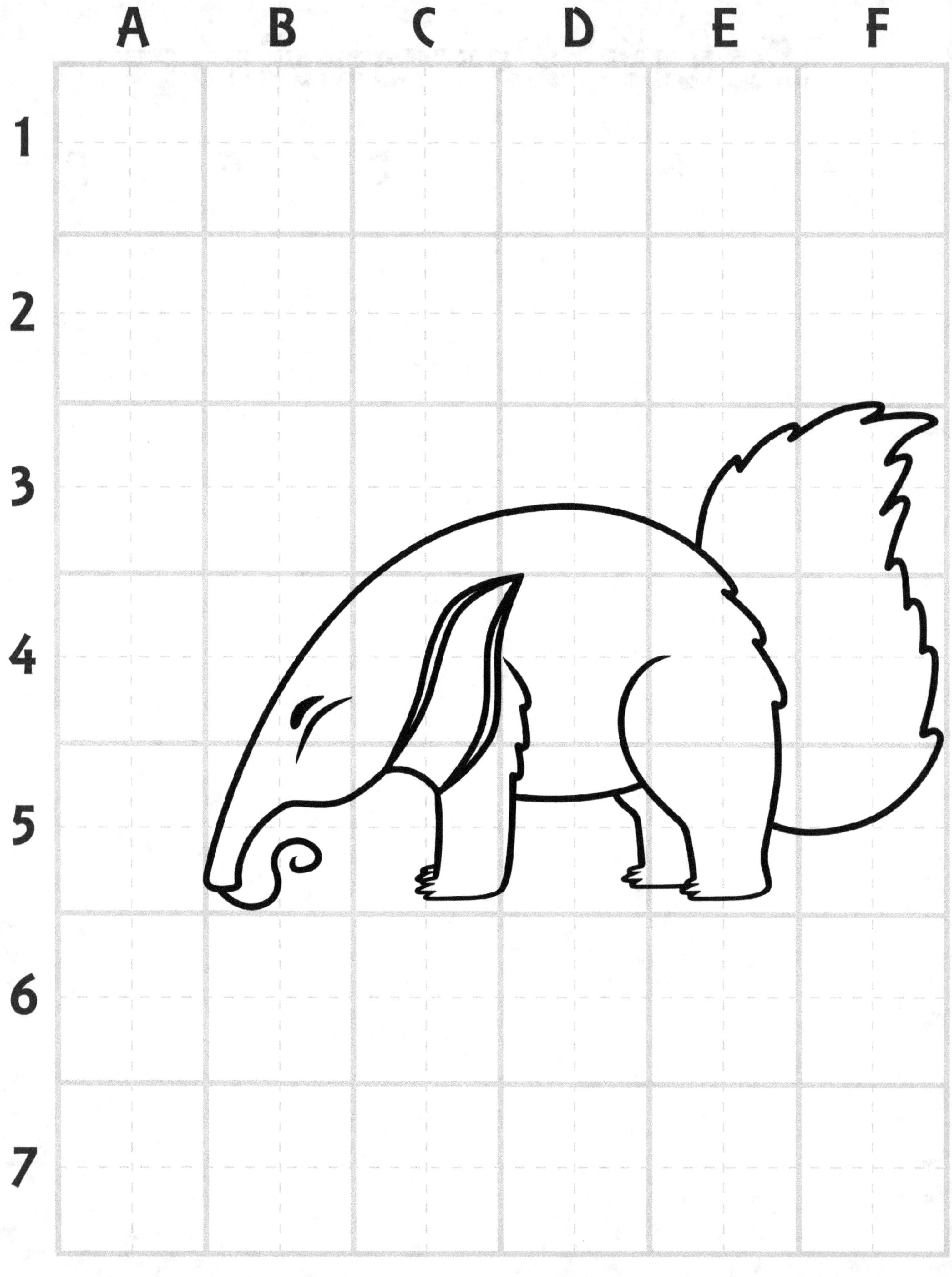

A B C D E F
1 2 3 4 5 6 7

Your Drawing

	A	B	C	D	E	F
1						
2						
3						
4						
5						
6						
7						

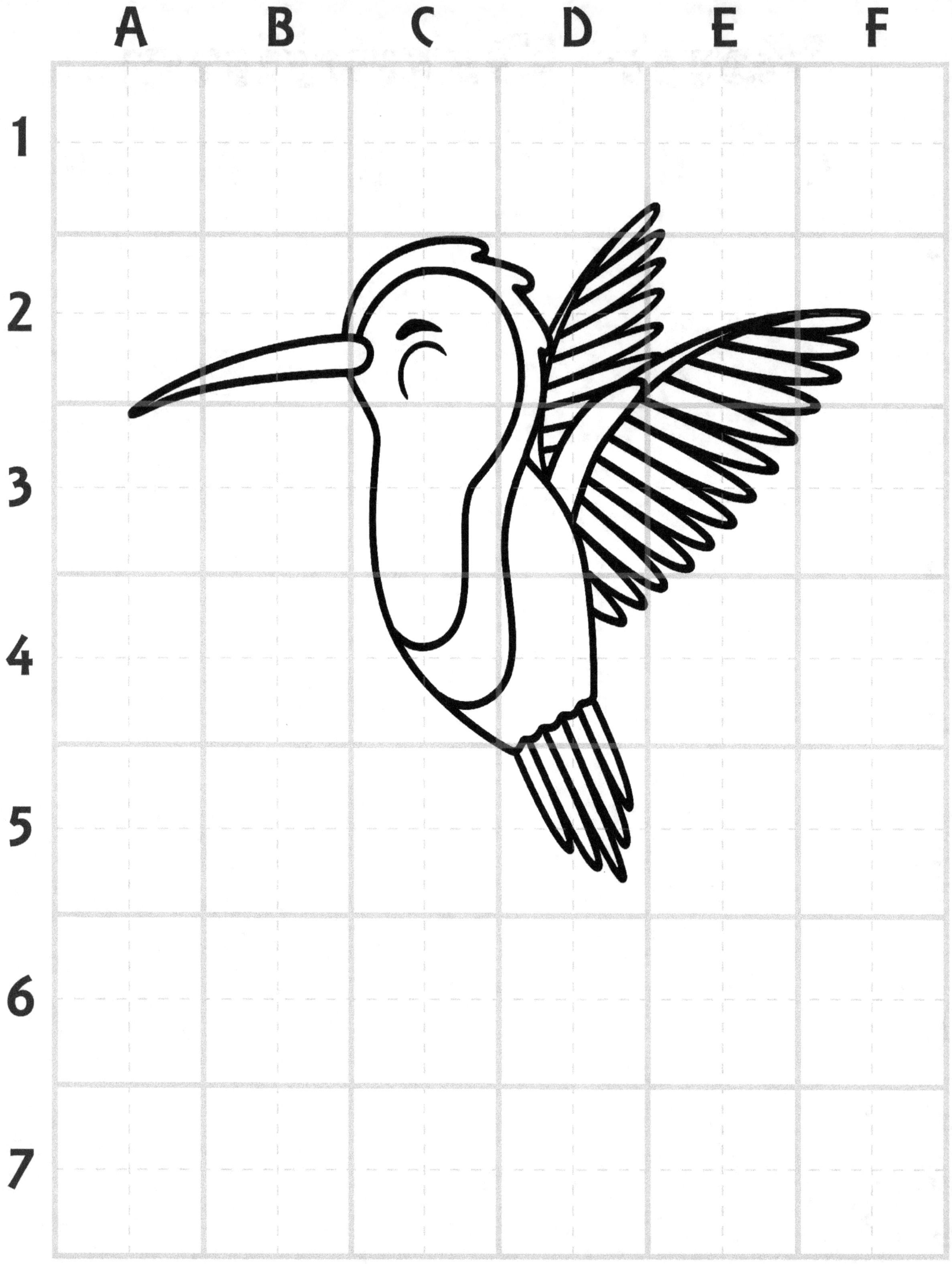
A B C D E F
1 2 3 4 5 6 7

Your Drawing

	A	B	C	D	E	F
1						
2						
3						
4						
5						
6						
7						

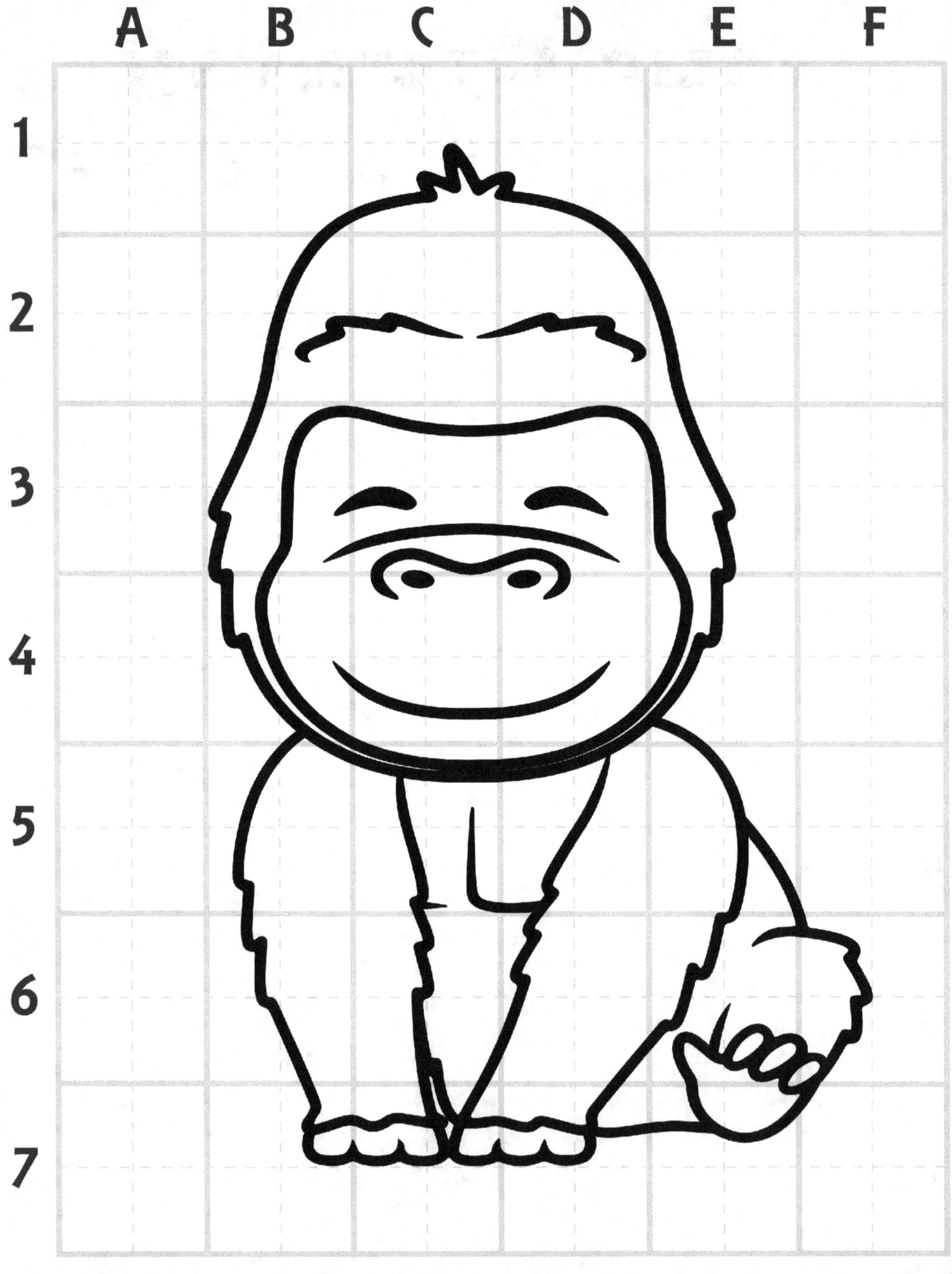
A B C D E F
1
2
3
4
5
6
7

Your Drawing

	A	B	C	D	E	F
1						
2						
3						
4						
5						
6						
7						

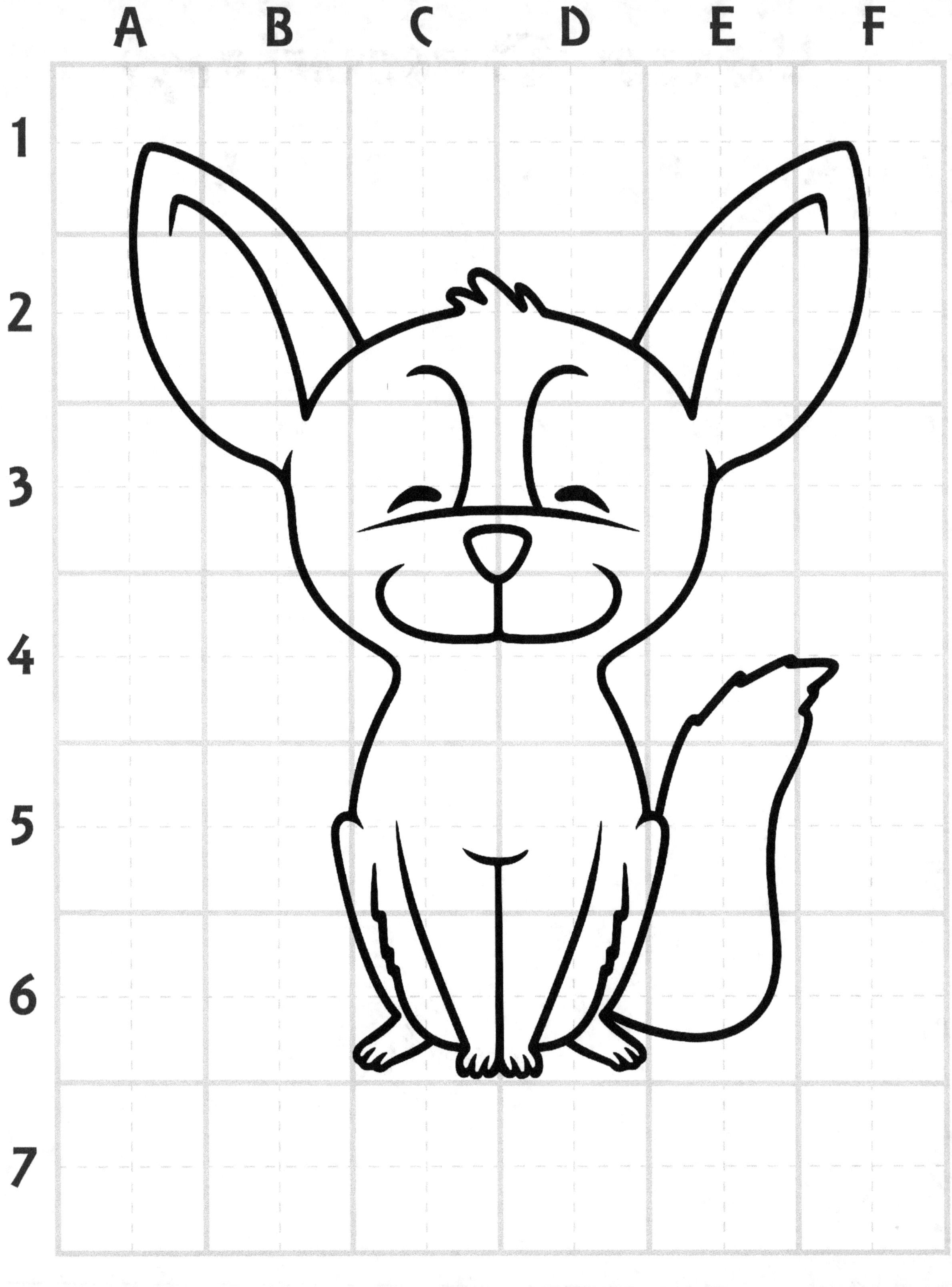
A B C D E F
1 2 3 4 5 6 7

Your Drawing

	A	B	C	D	E	F
1						
2						
3						
4						
5						
6						
7						

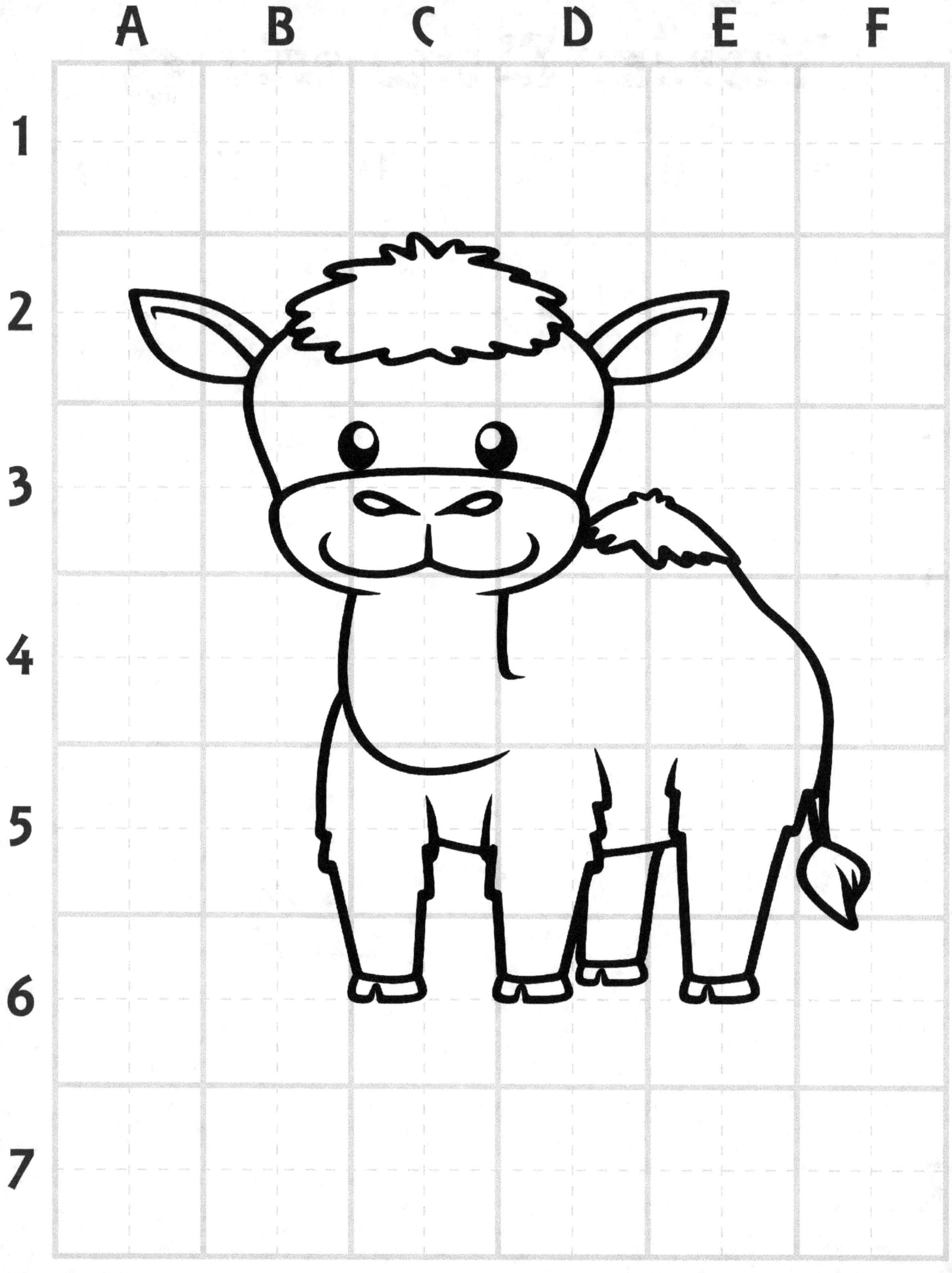
A
B
C
D
E
F
1
2
3
4
5
6
7

Your Drawing

	A	B	C	D	E	F
1						
2						
3						
4						
5						
6						
7						

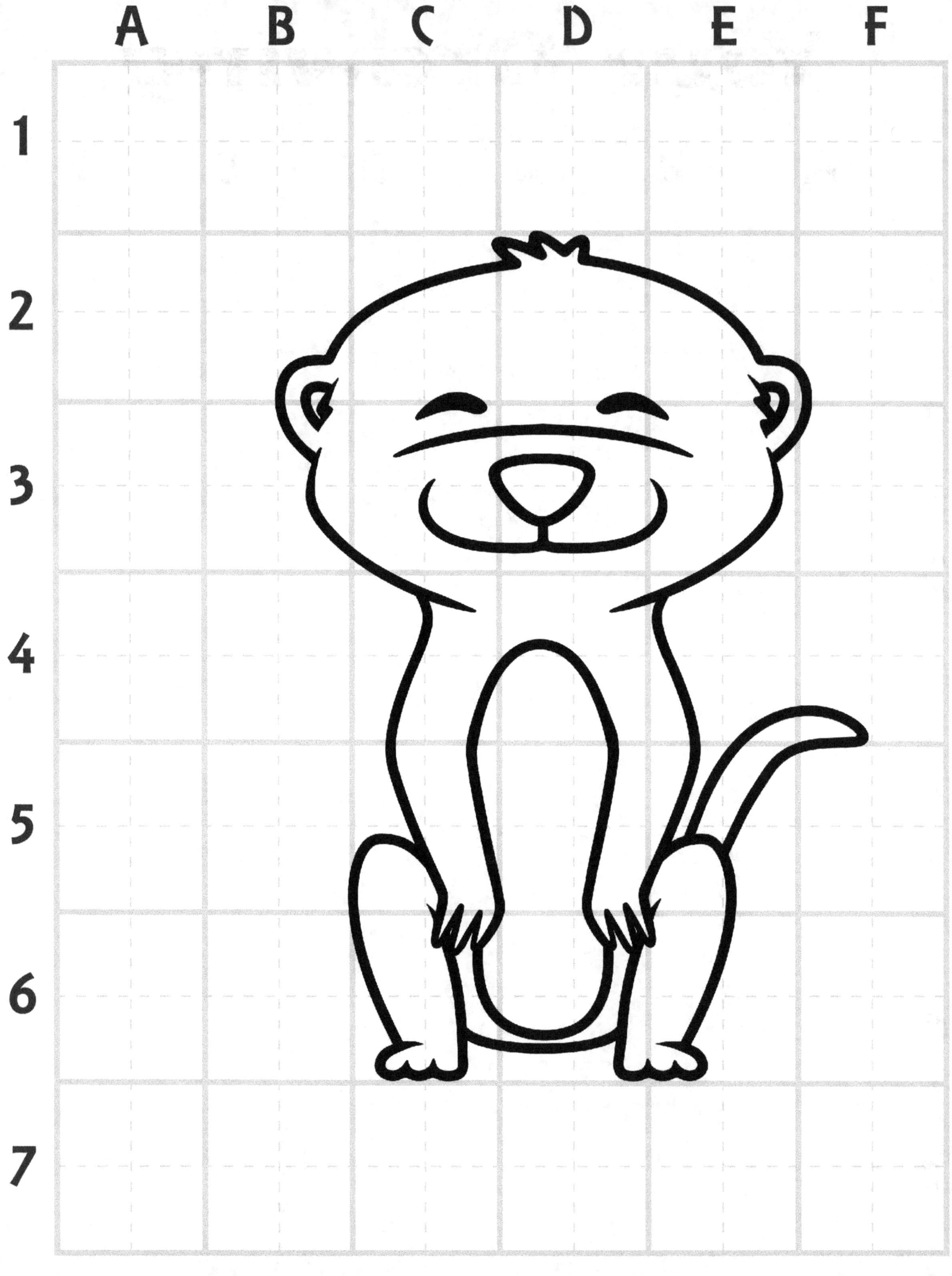
A B C D E F
1 2 3 4 5 6 7

Your Drawing

	A	B	C	D	E	F
1						
2						
3						
4						
5						
6						
7						

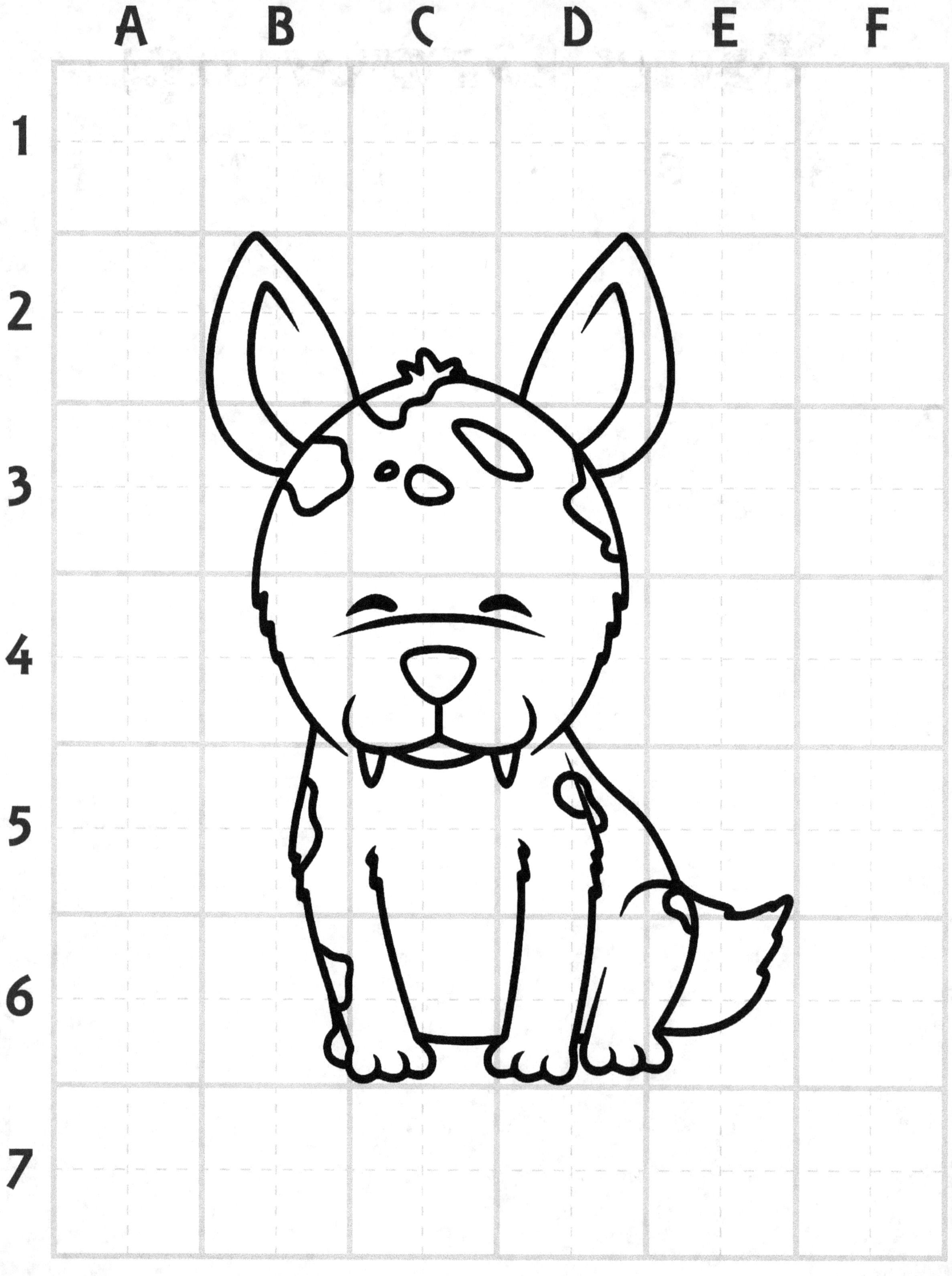

Your Drawing

	A	B	C	D	E	F
1						
2						
3						
4						
5						
6						
7						

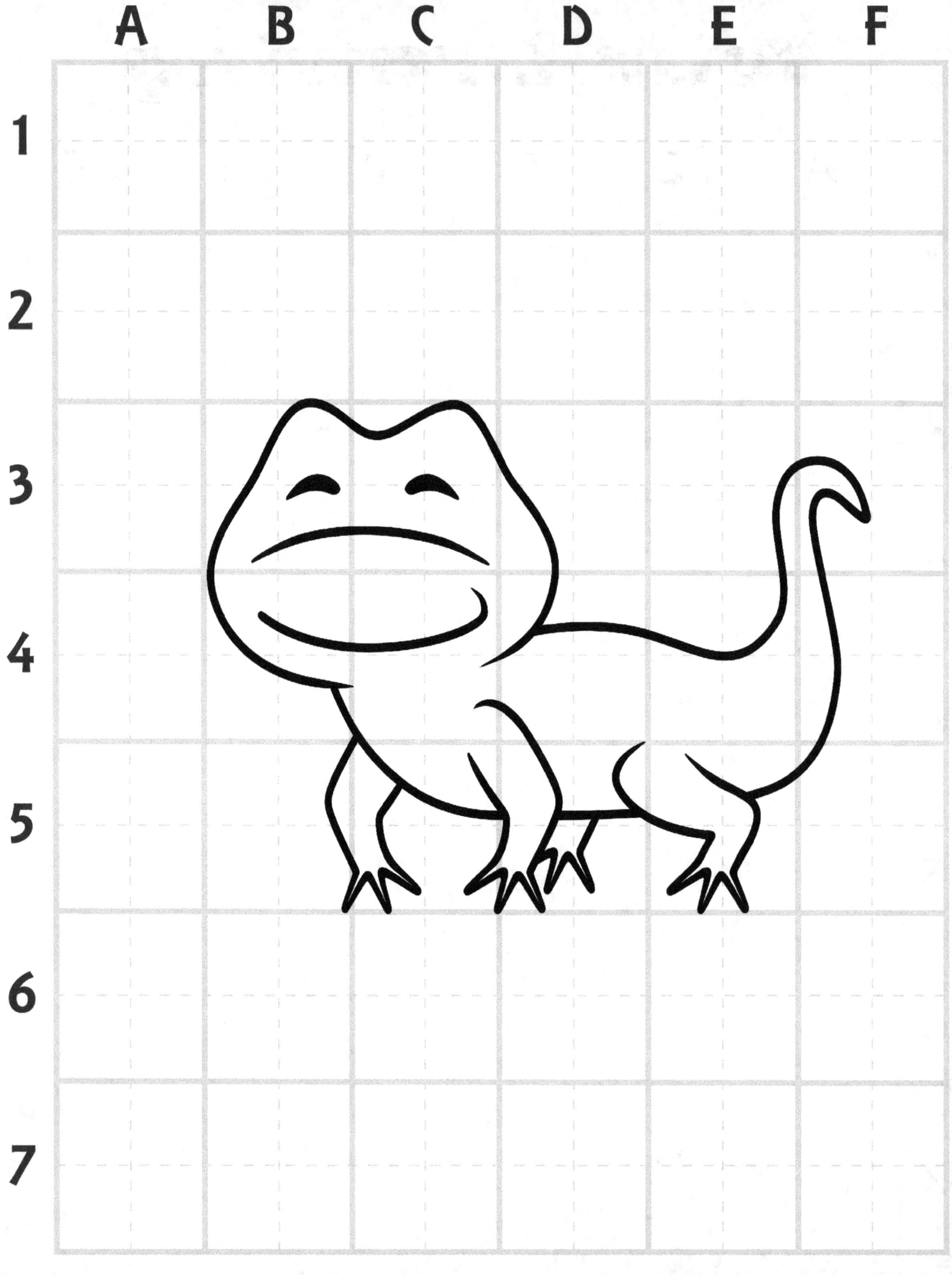
A
B
C
D
E
F
1
2
3
4
5
6
7

Your Drawing

	A	B	C	D	E	F
1						
2						
3						
4						
5						
6						
7						

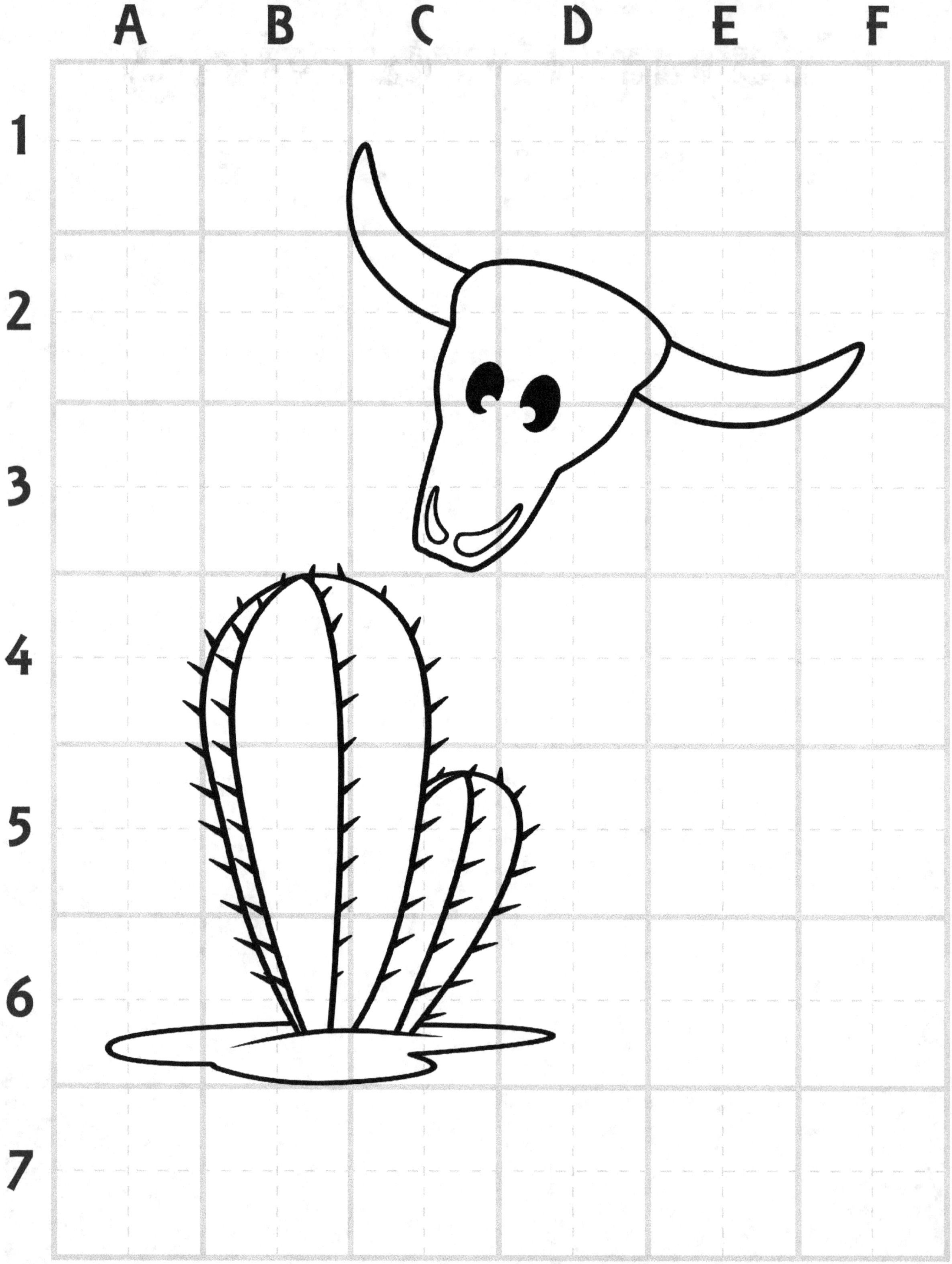
A
B
C
D
E
F
1
2
3
4
5
6
7

Your Drawing

	A	B	C	D	E	F
1						
2						
3						
4						
5						
6						
7						

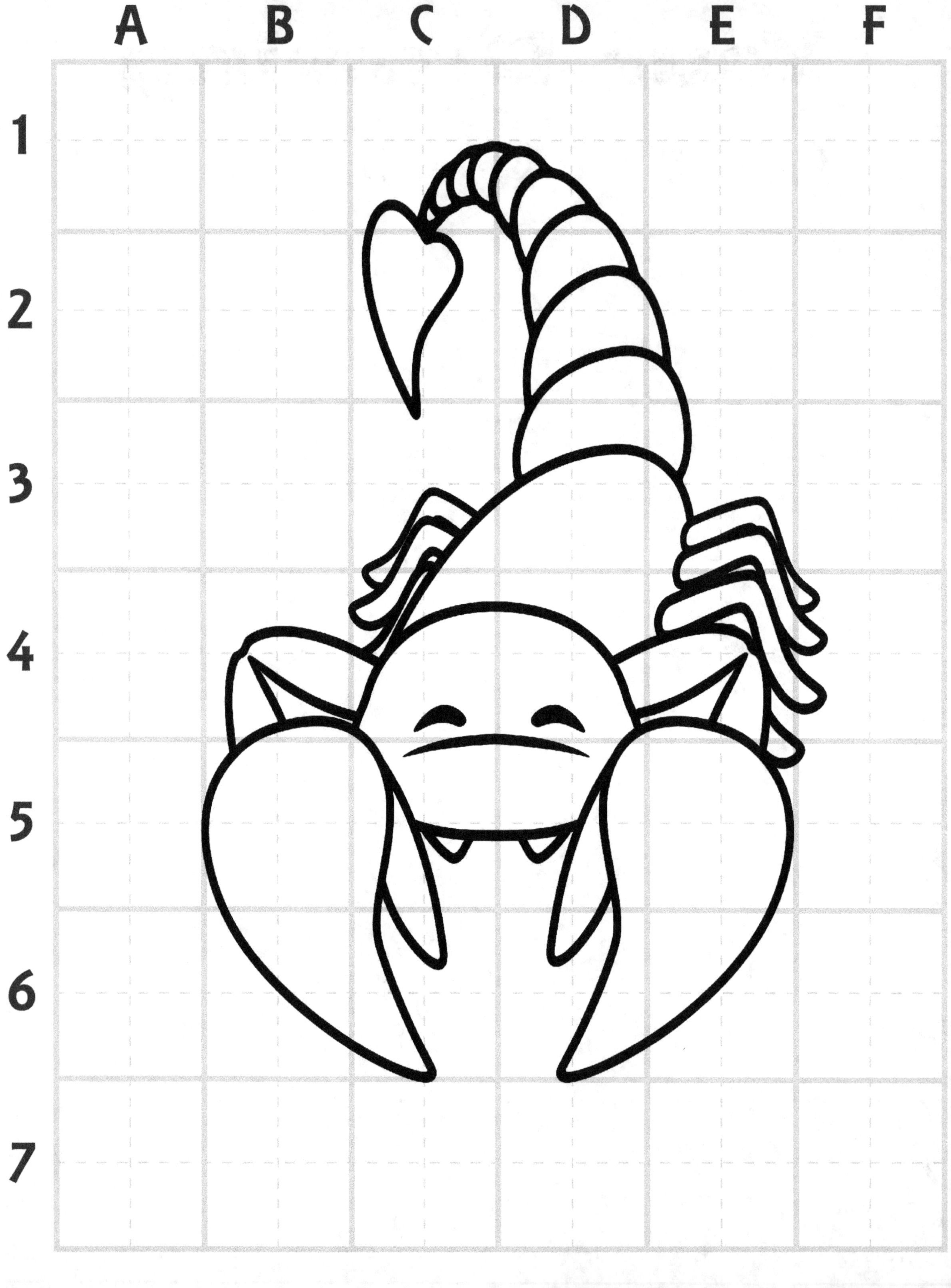
A
B
C
D
E
F
1
2
3
4
5
6
7

Your Drawing

	A	B	C	D	E	F
1						
2						
3						
4						
5						
6						
7						

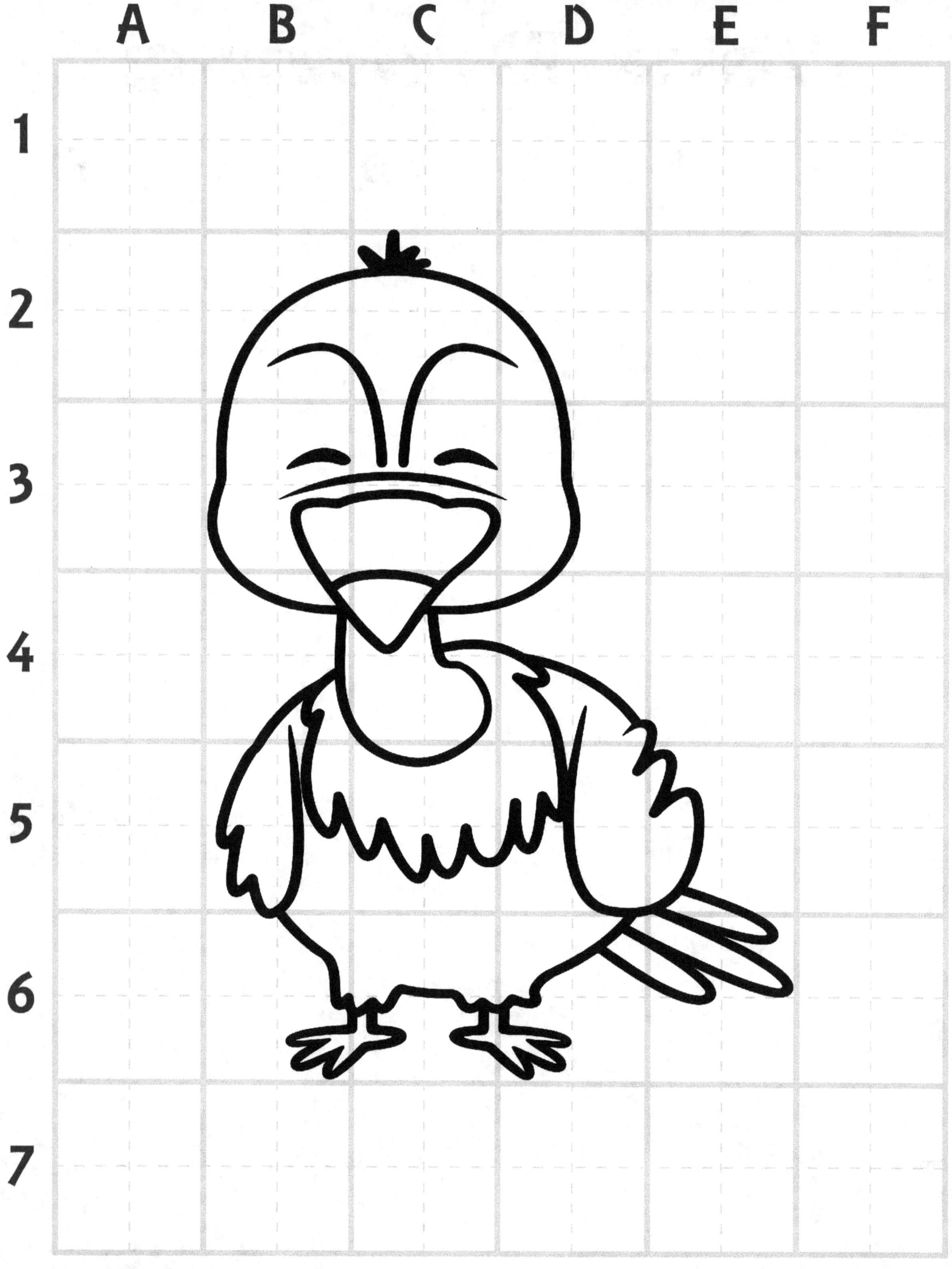
A B C D E F
1
2
3
4
5
6
7

Your Drawing

	A	B	C	D	E	F
1						
2						
3						
4						
5						
6						
7						

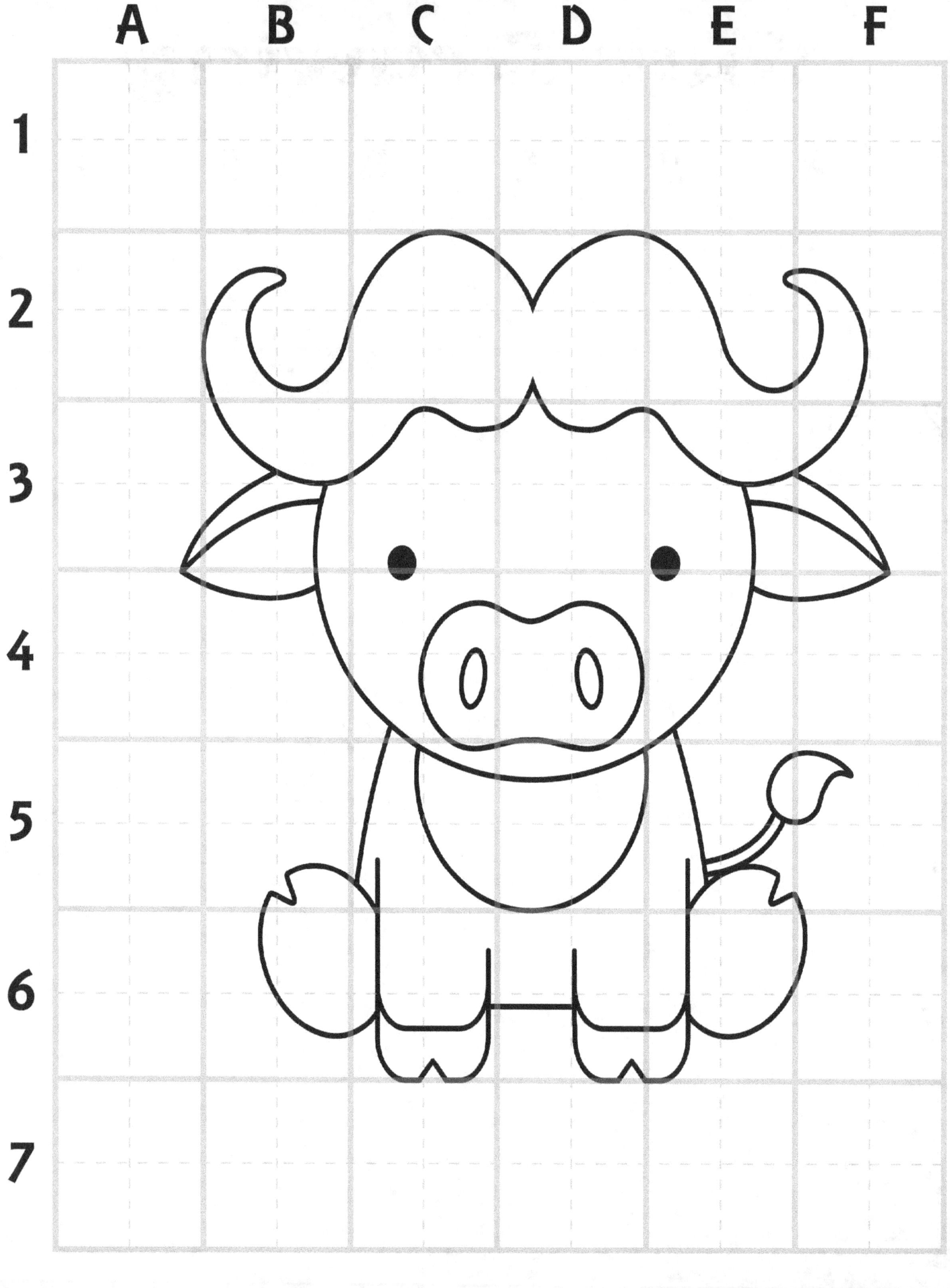
A B C D E F
1
2
3
4
5
6
7

Your Drawing

	A	B	C	D	E	F
1						
2						
3						
4						
5						
6						
7						

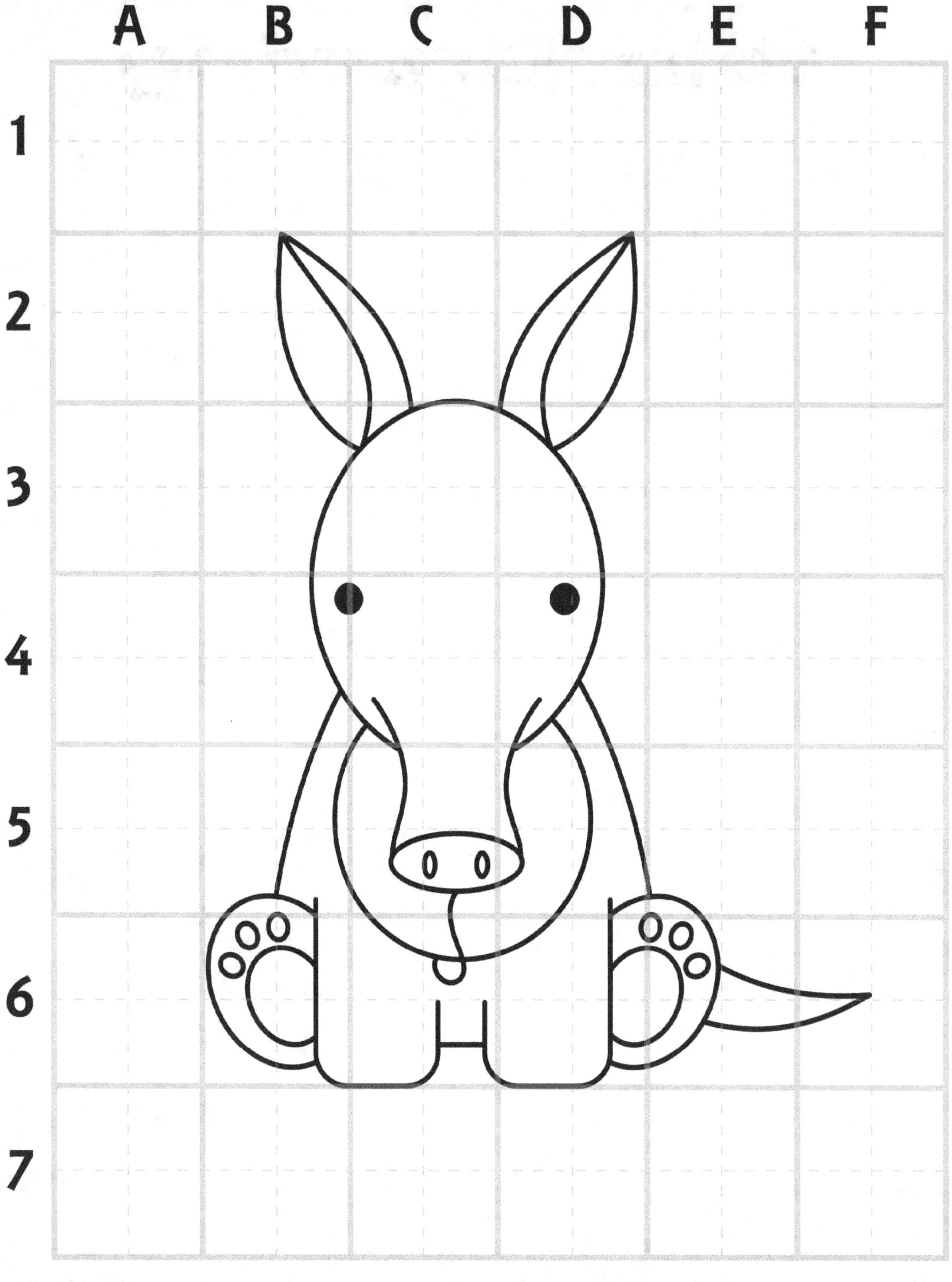
A B C D E F
1
2
3
4
5
6
7

Your Drawing

	A	B	C	D	E	F
1						
2						
3						
4						
5						
6						
7						

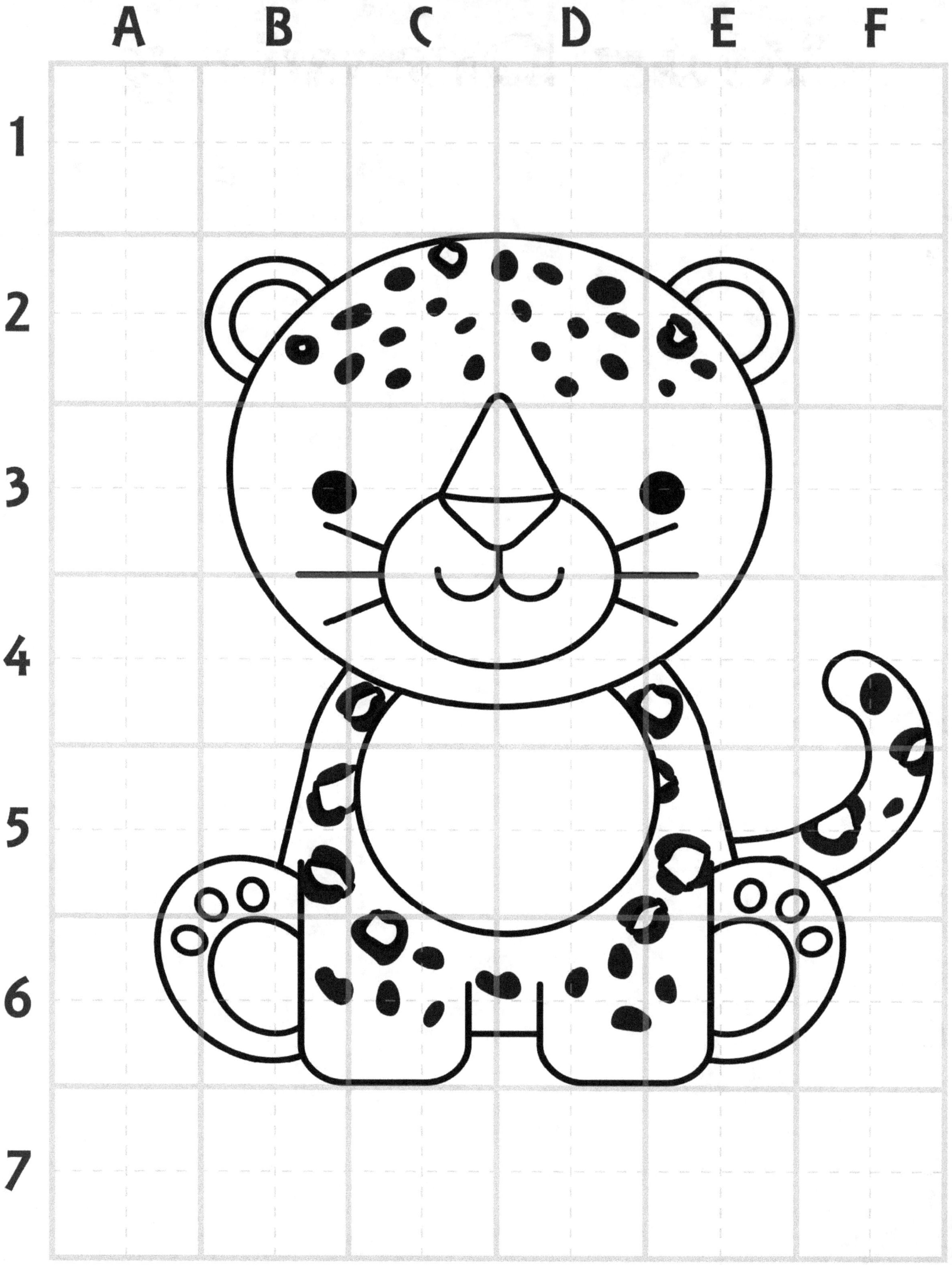
A B C D E F
1 2 3 4 5 6 7

Your Drawing

	A	B	C	D	E	F
1						
2						
3						
4						
5						
6						
7						

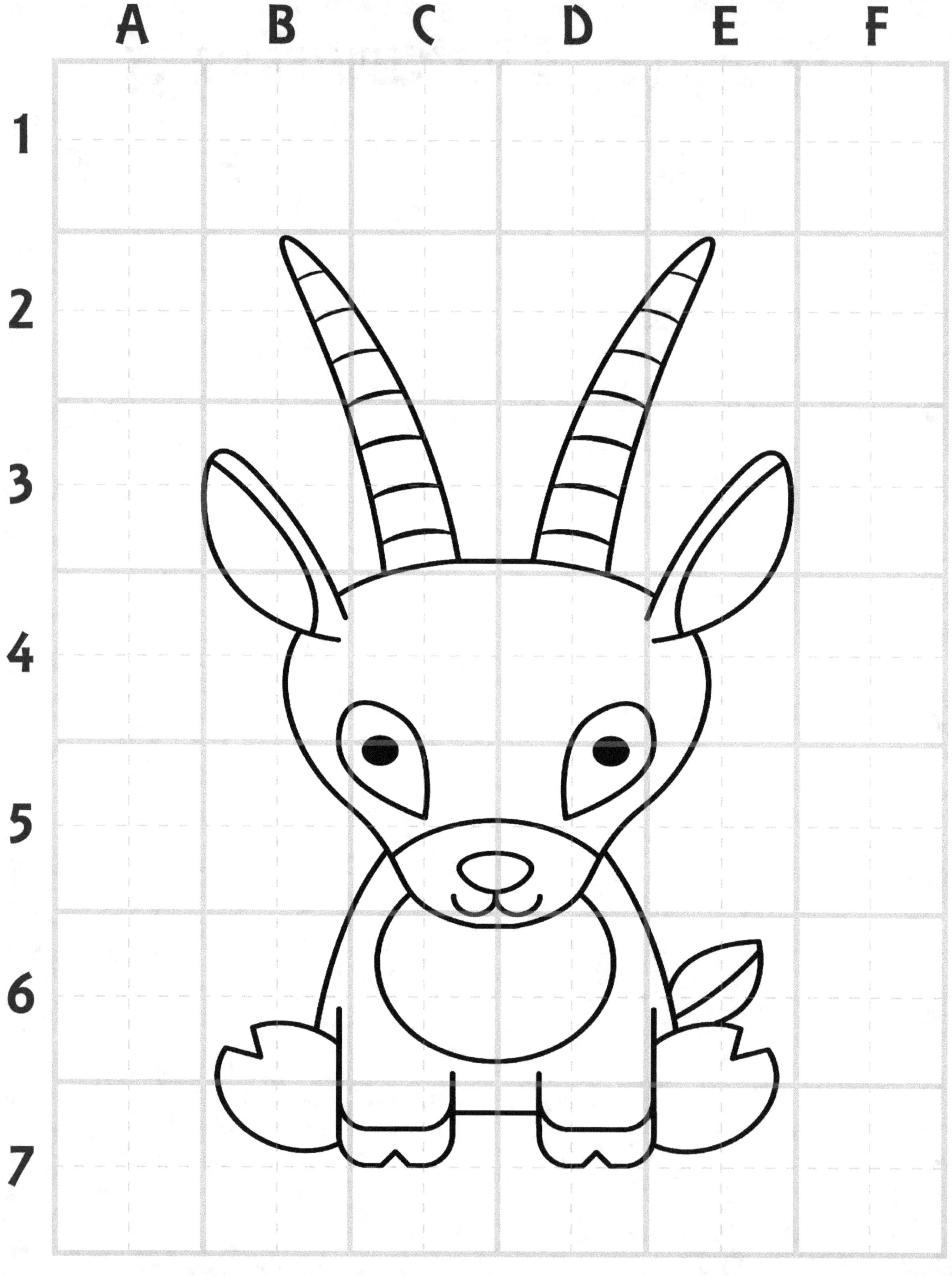
A B C D E F
1 2 3 4 5 6 7

Your Drawing

	A	B	C	D	E	F
1						
2						
3						
4						
5						
6						
7						

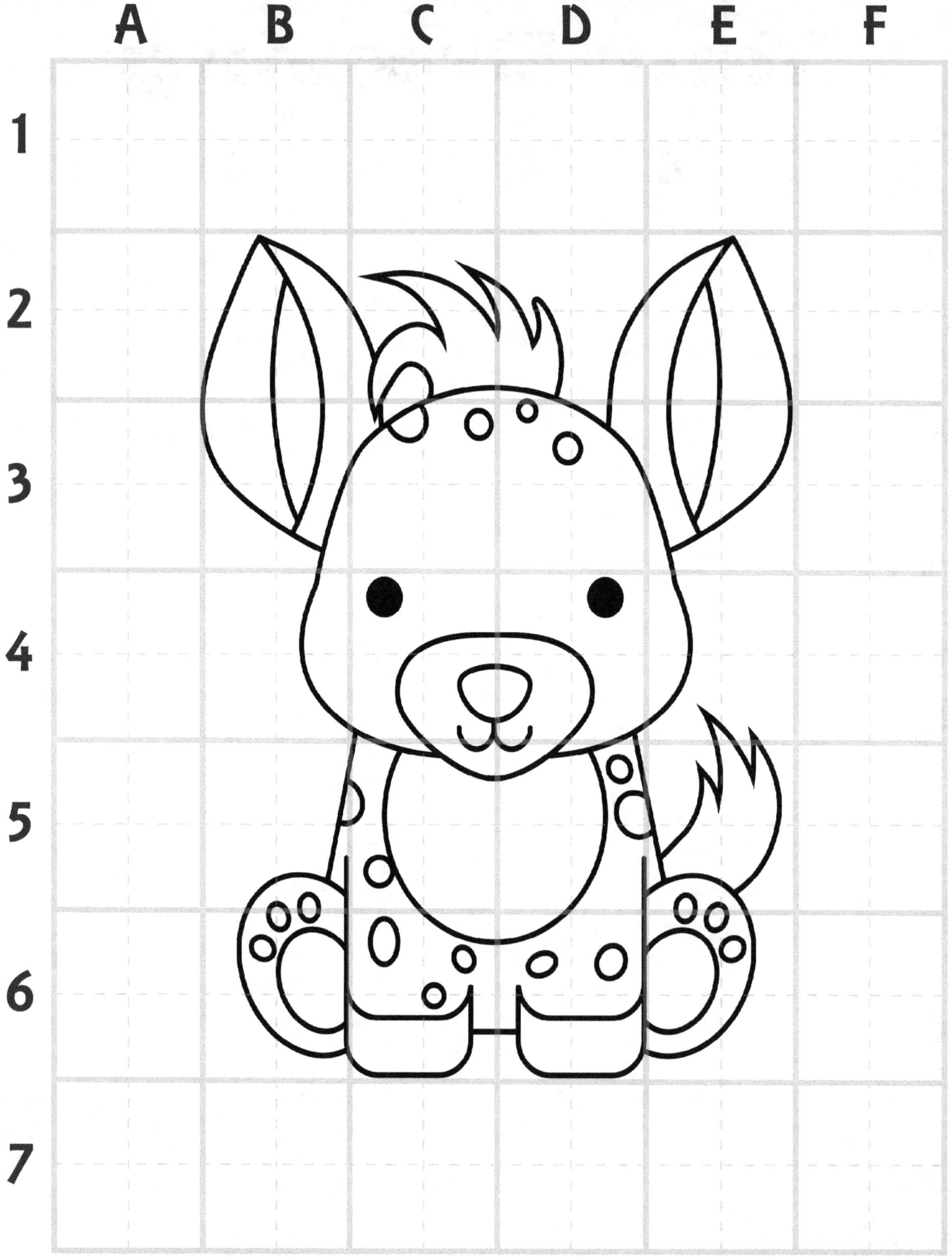
A
B
C
D
E
F
1
2
3
4
5
6
7

Your Drawing

	A	B	C	D	E	F
1						
2						
3						
4						
5						
6						
7						

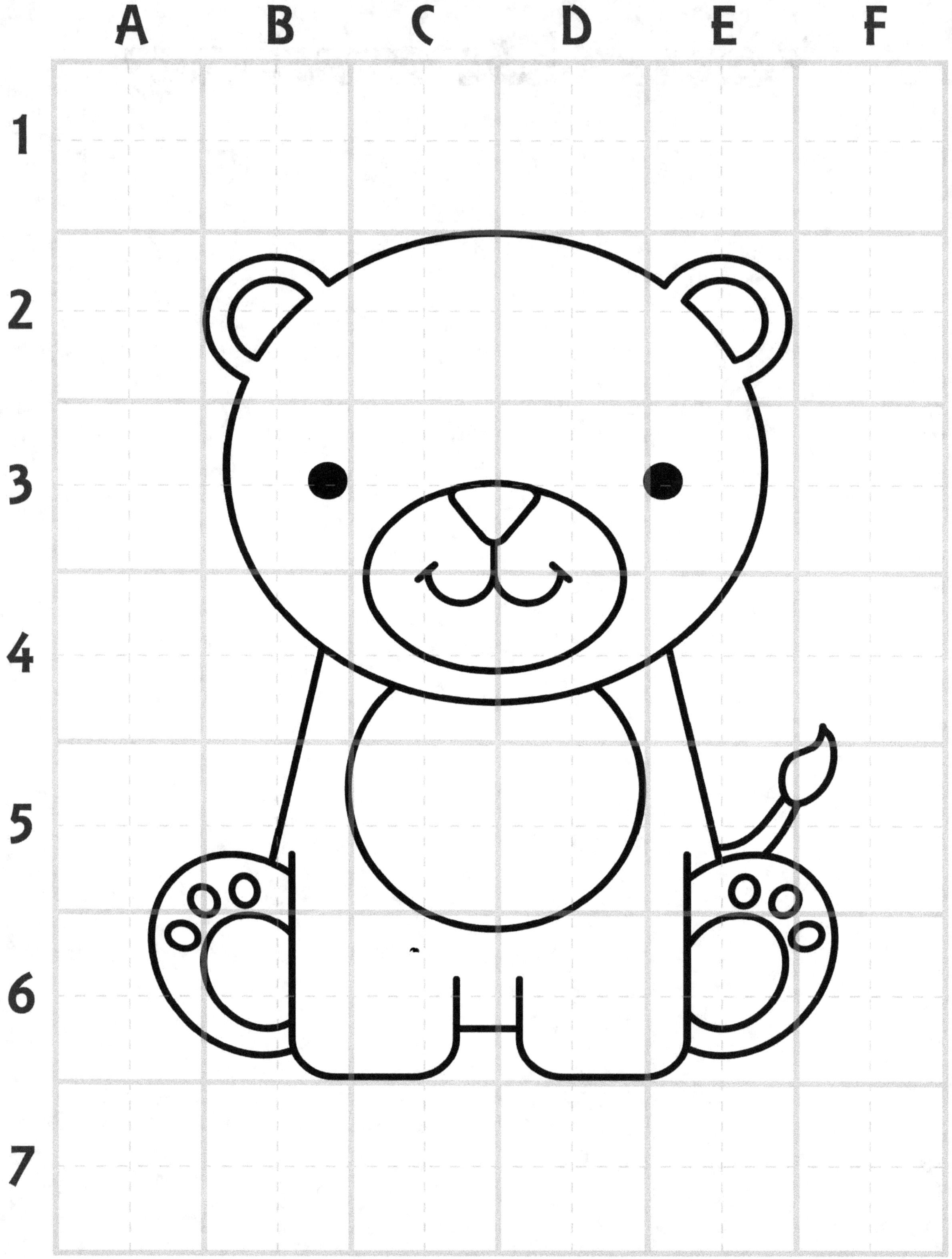
A
B
C
D
E
F
1
2
3
4
5
6
7

Your Drawing

	A	B	C	D	E	F
1						
2						
3						
4						
5						
6						
7						

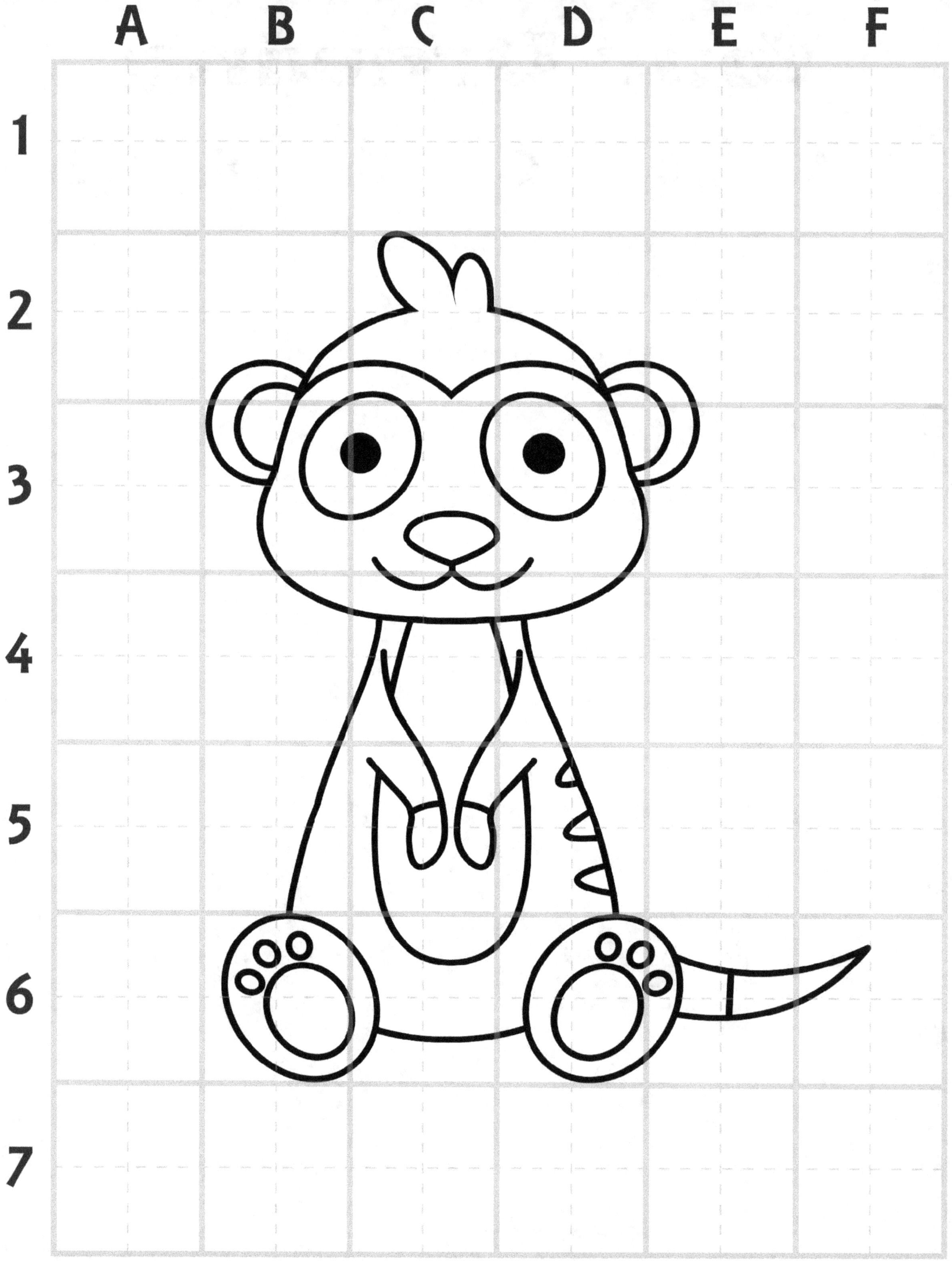
A
B
C
D
E
F
1
2
3
4
5
6
7

Your Drawing

	A	B	C	D	E	F
1						
2						
3						
4						
5						
6						
7						

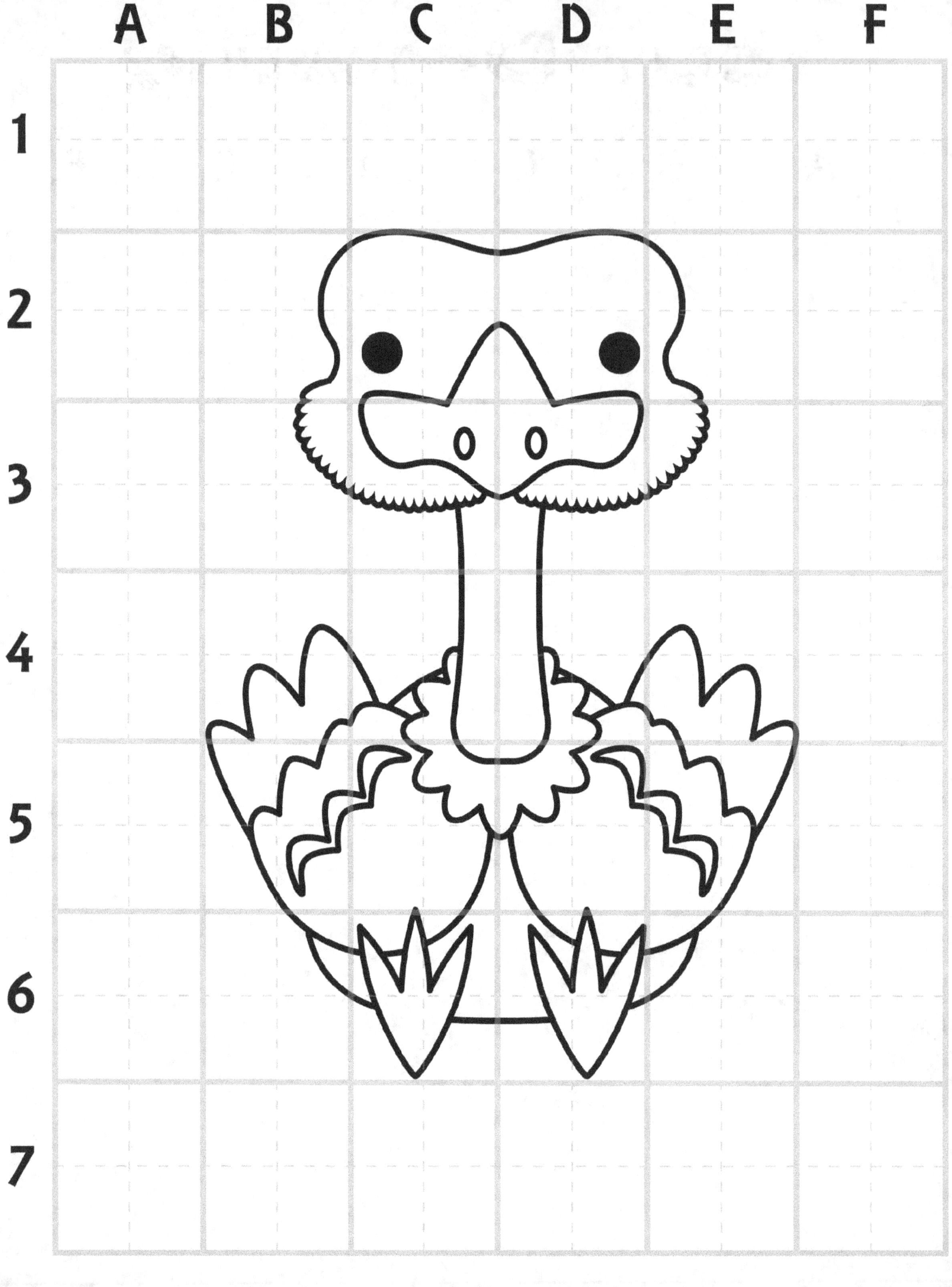
A B C D E F
1
2
3
4
5
6
7

Your Drawing

	A	B	C	D	E	F
1						
2						
3						
4						
5						
6						
7						

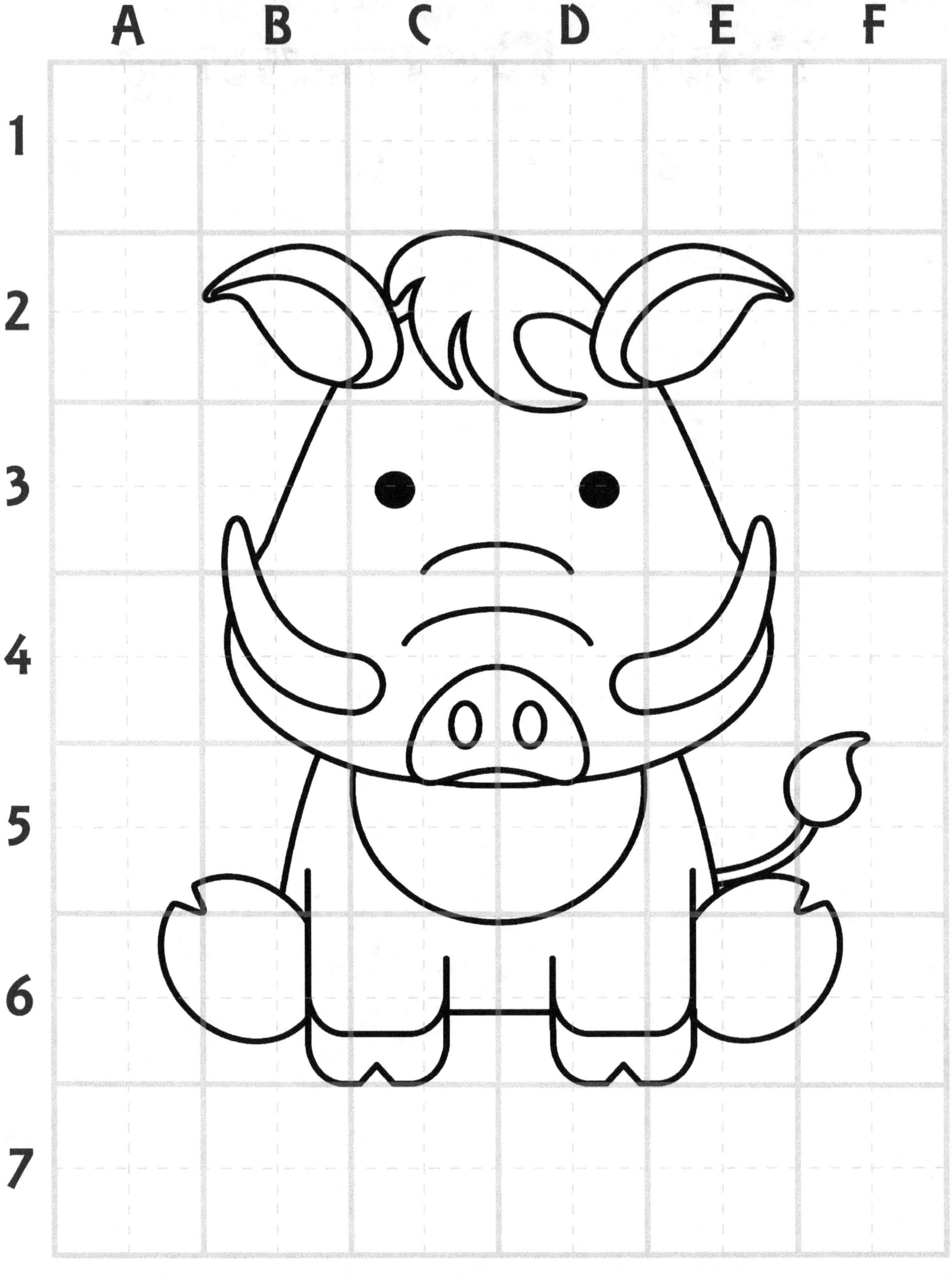
A
B
C
D
E
F
1
2
3
4
5
6
7

Your Drawing

	A	B	C	D	E	F
1						
2						
3						
4						
5						
6						
7						

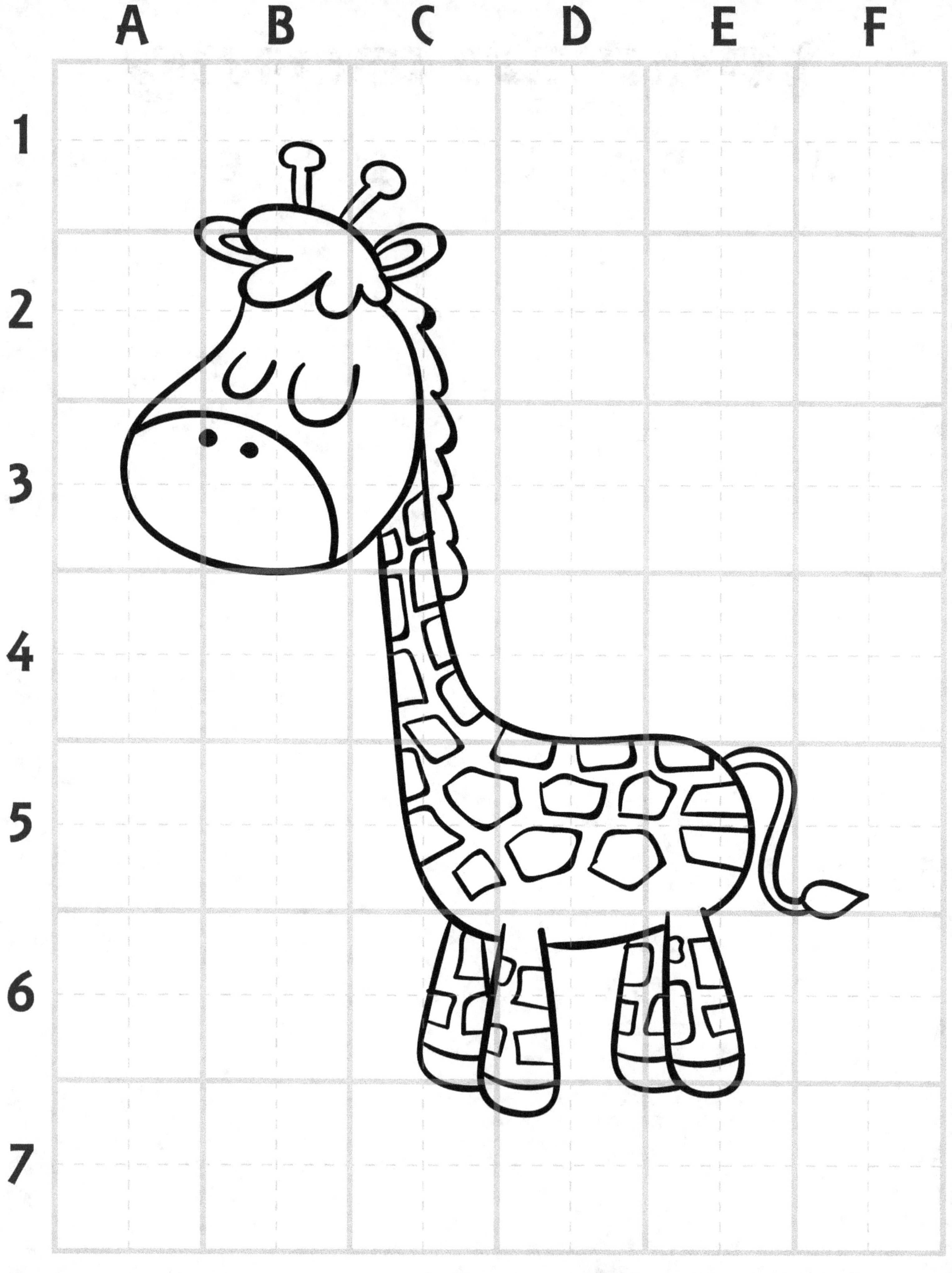
A
B
C
D
E
F
1
2
3
4
5
6
7

Your Drawing

	A	B	C	D	E	F
1						
2						
3						
4						
5						
6						
7						

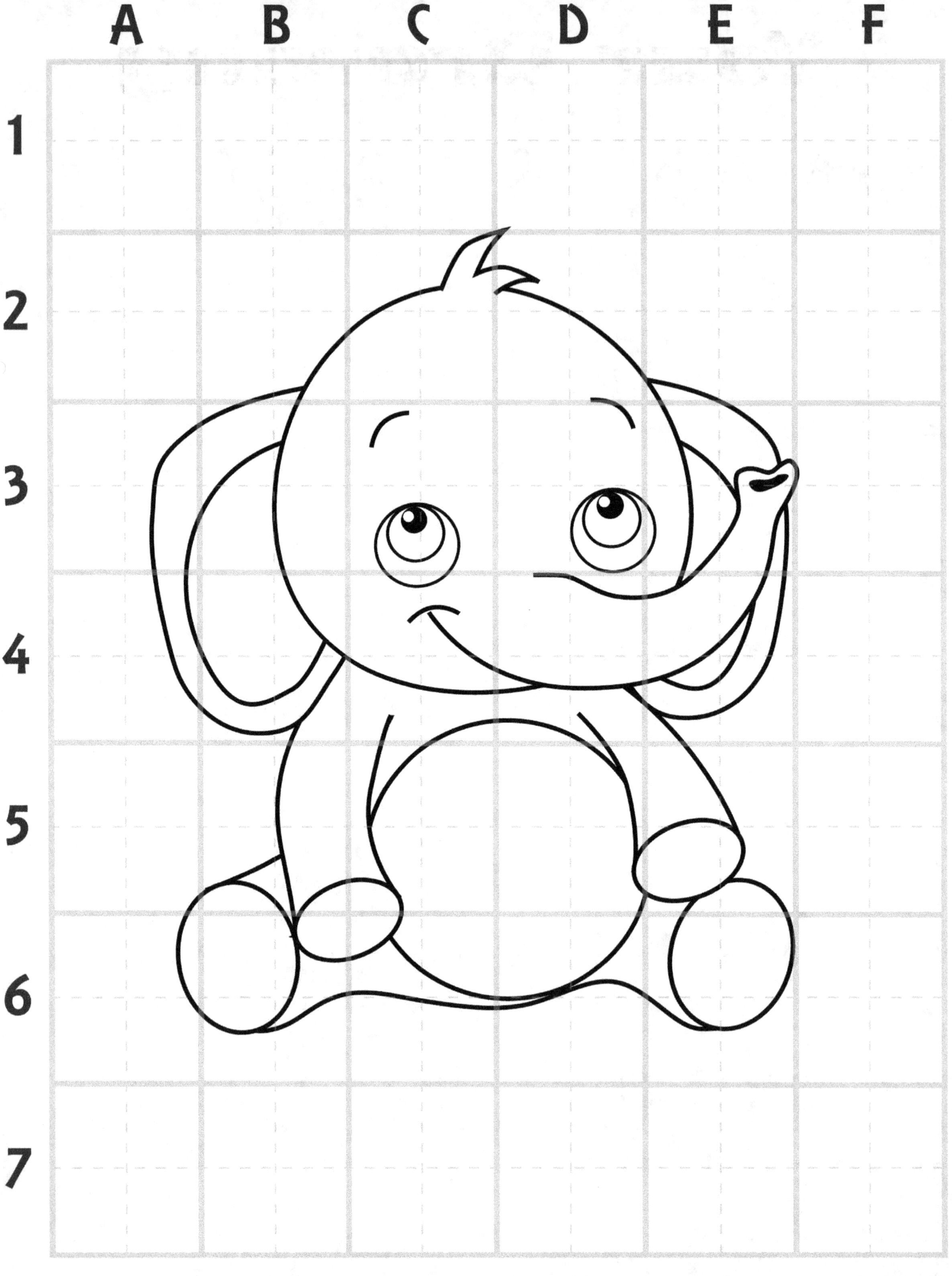
A B C D E F
1
2
3
4
5
6
7

Your Drawing

	A	B	C	D	E	F
1						
2						
3						
4						
5						
6						
7						

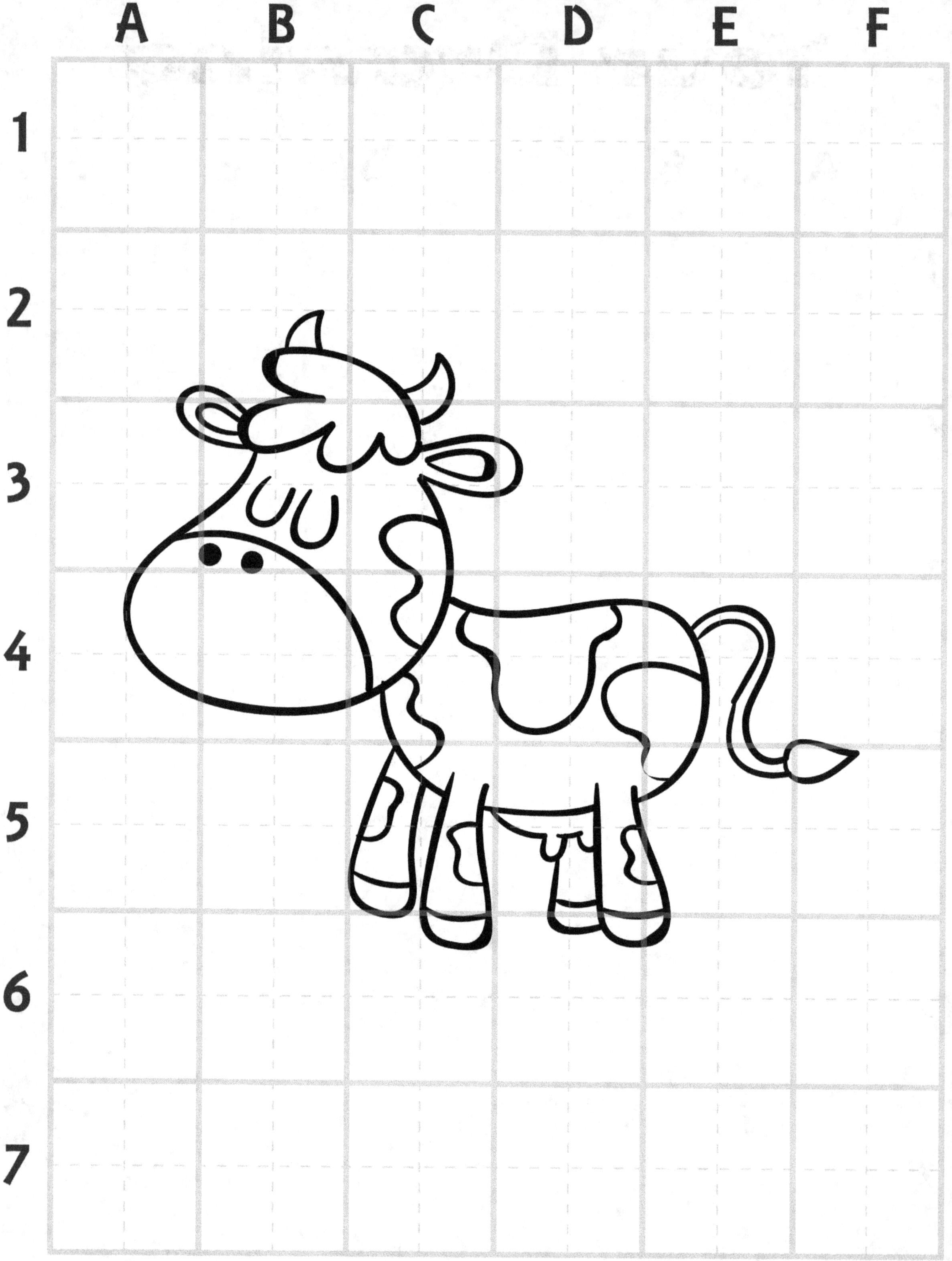
A
B
C
D
E
F
1
2
3
4
5
6
7

Your Drawing

	A	B	C	D	E	F
1						
2						
3						
4						
5						
6						
7						

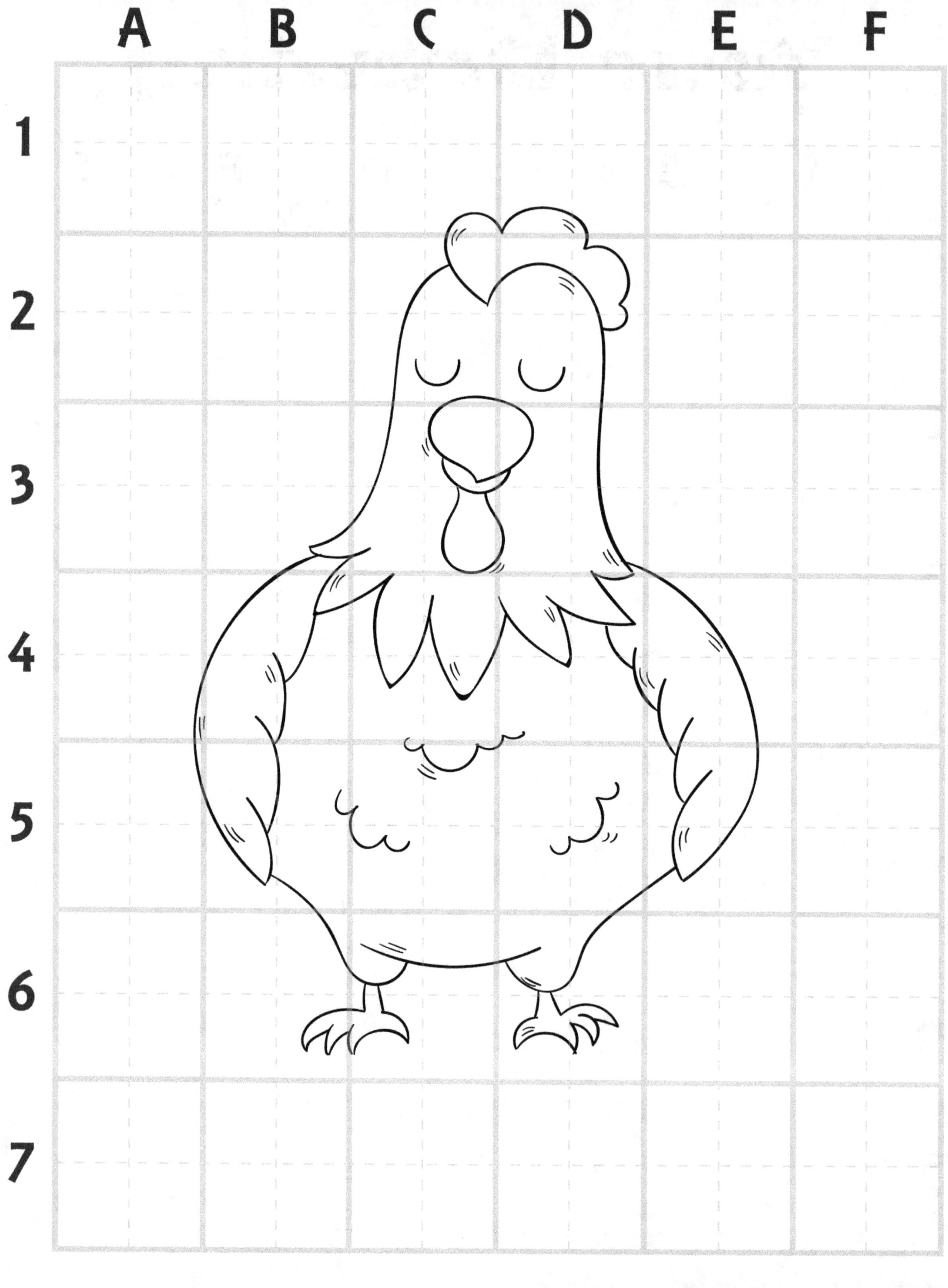
A
B
C
D
E
F
1
2
3
4
5
6
7

Your Drawing

	A	B	C	D	E	F
1						
2						
3						
4						
5						
6						
7						

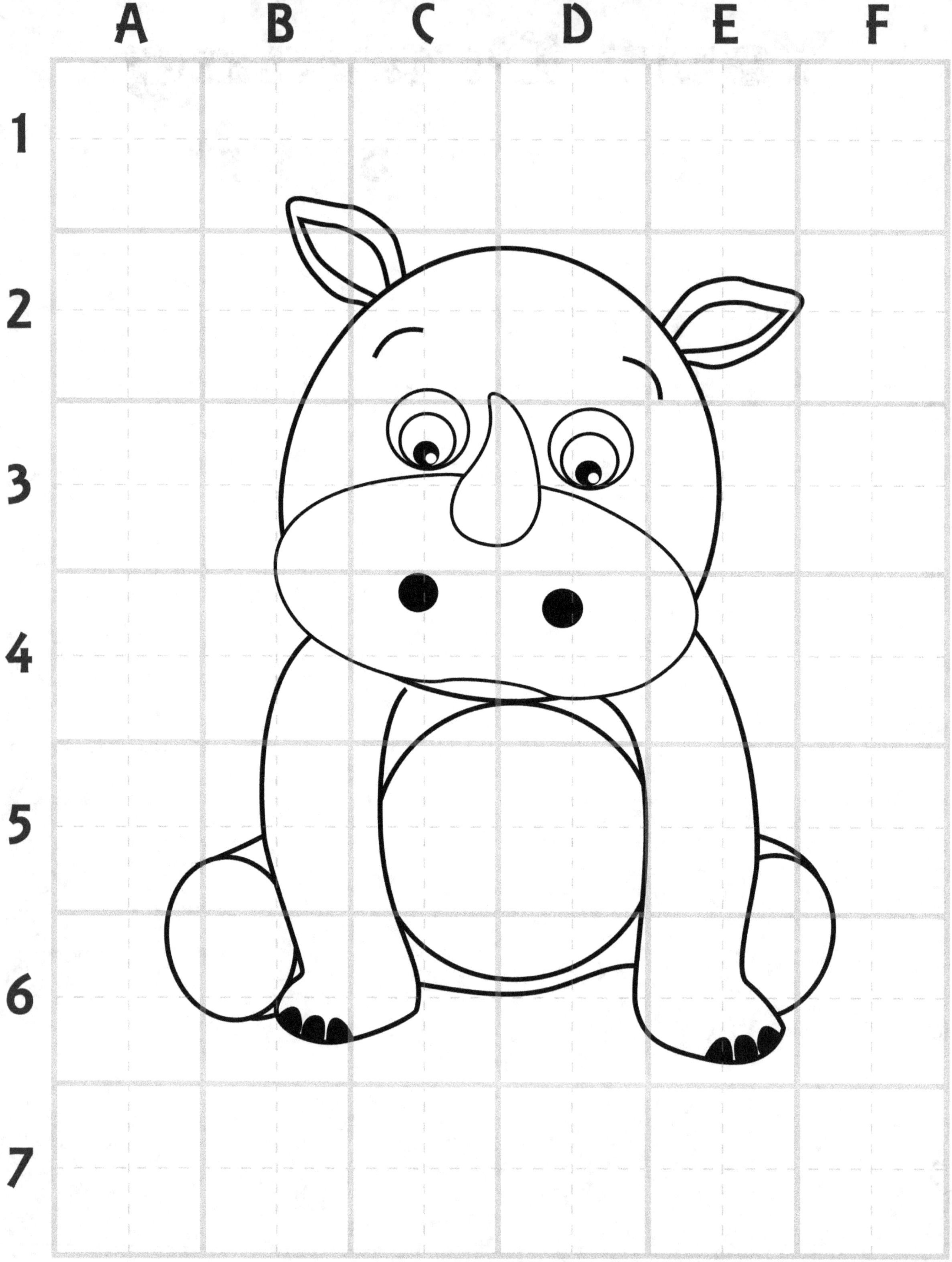
A B C D E F
1 2 3 4 5 6 7

Your Drawing

	A	B	C	D	E	F
1						
2						
3						
4						
5						
6						
7						

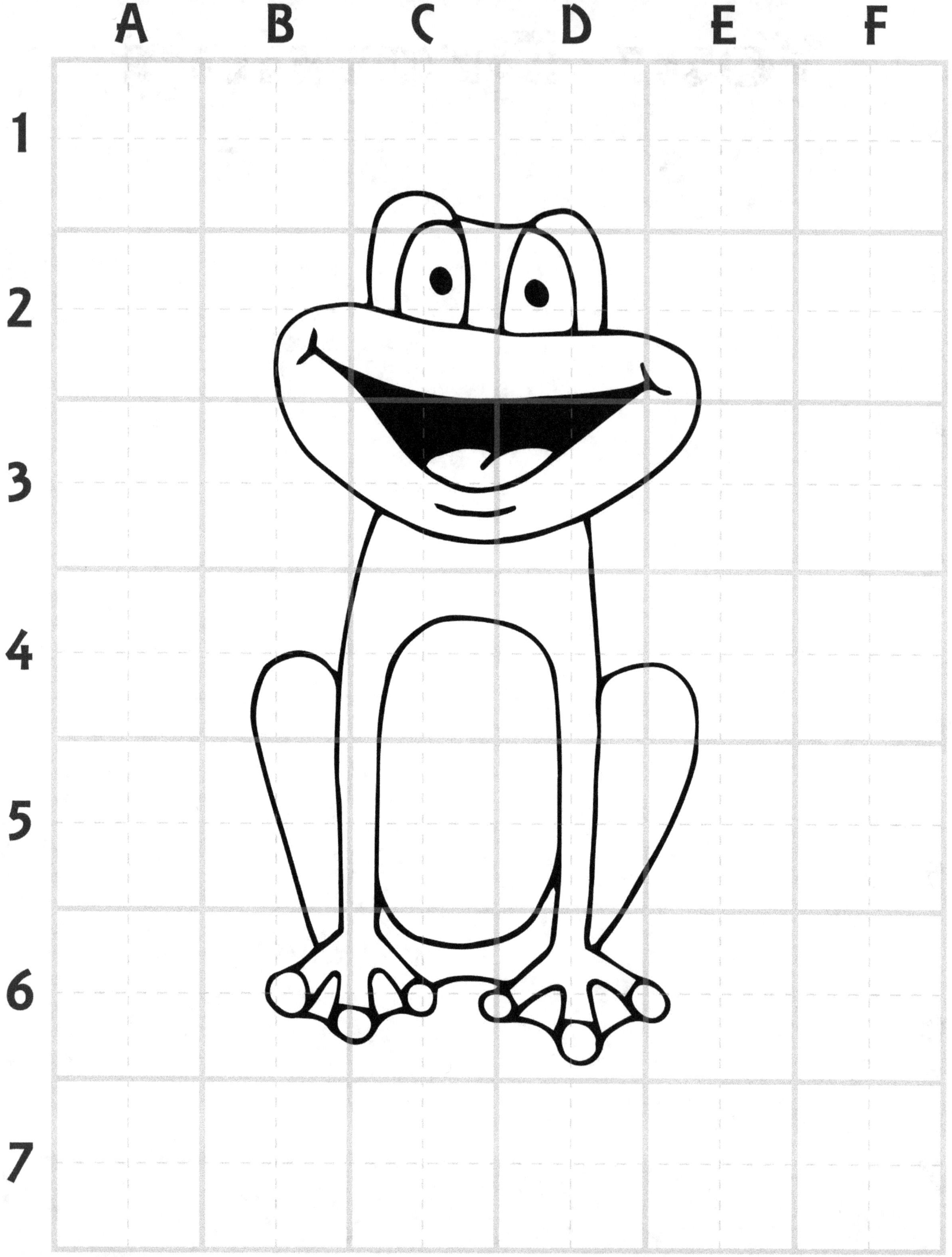
A B C D E F
1 2 3 4 5 6 7

Your Drawing

	A	B	C	D	E	F
1						
2						
3						
4						
5						
6						
7						

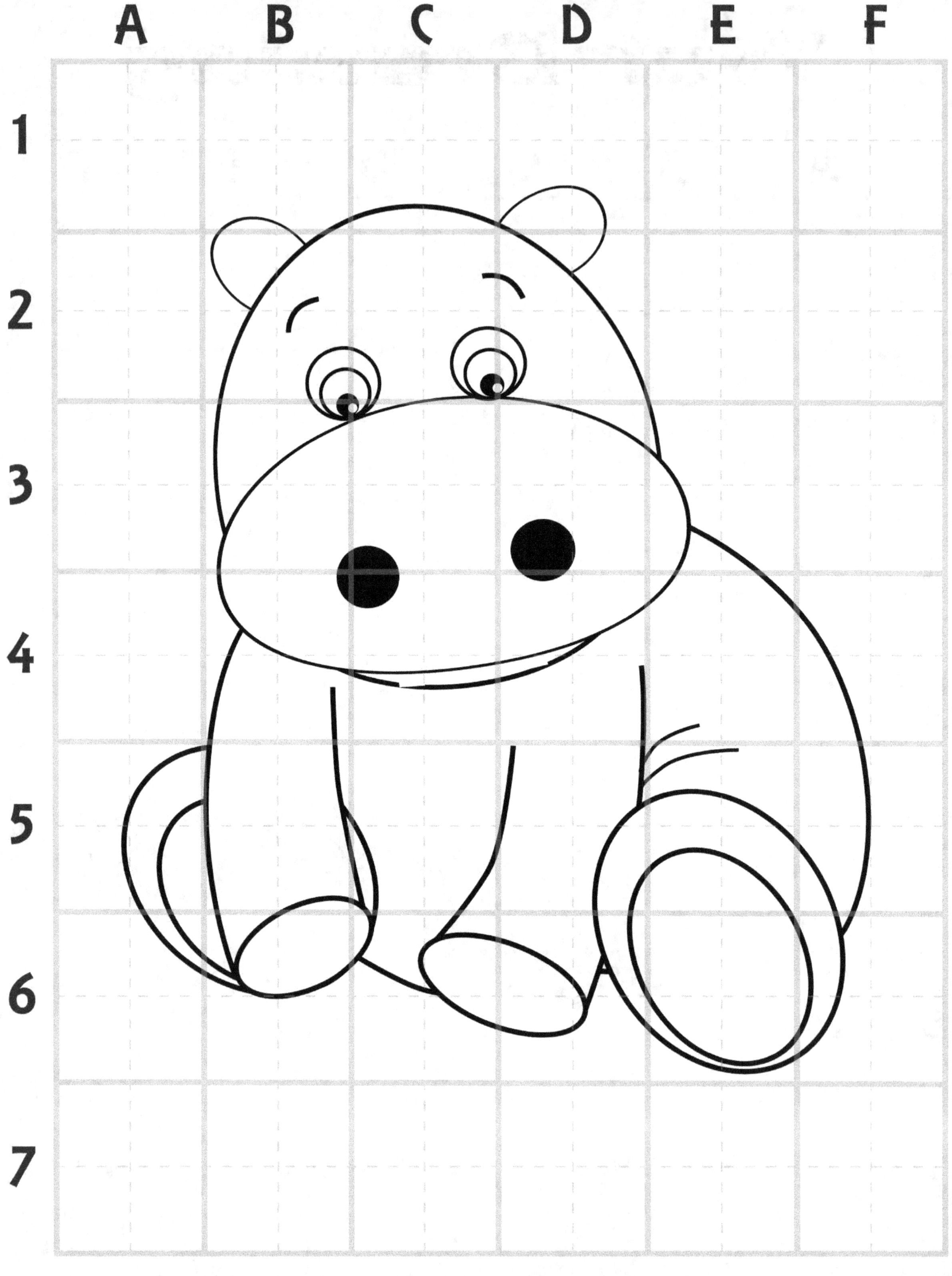
A B C D E F
1
2
3
4
5
6
7

Your Drawing

	A	B	C	D	E	F
1						
2						
3						
4						
5						
6						
7						

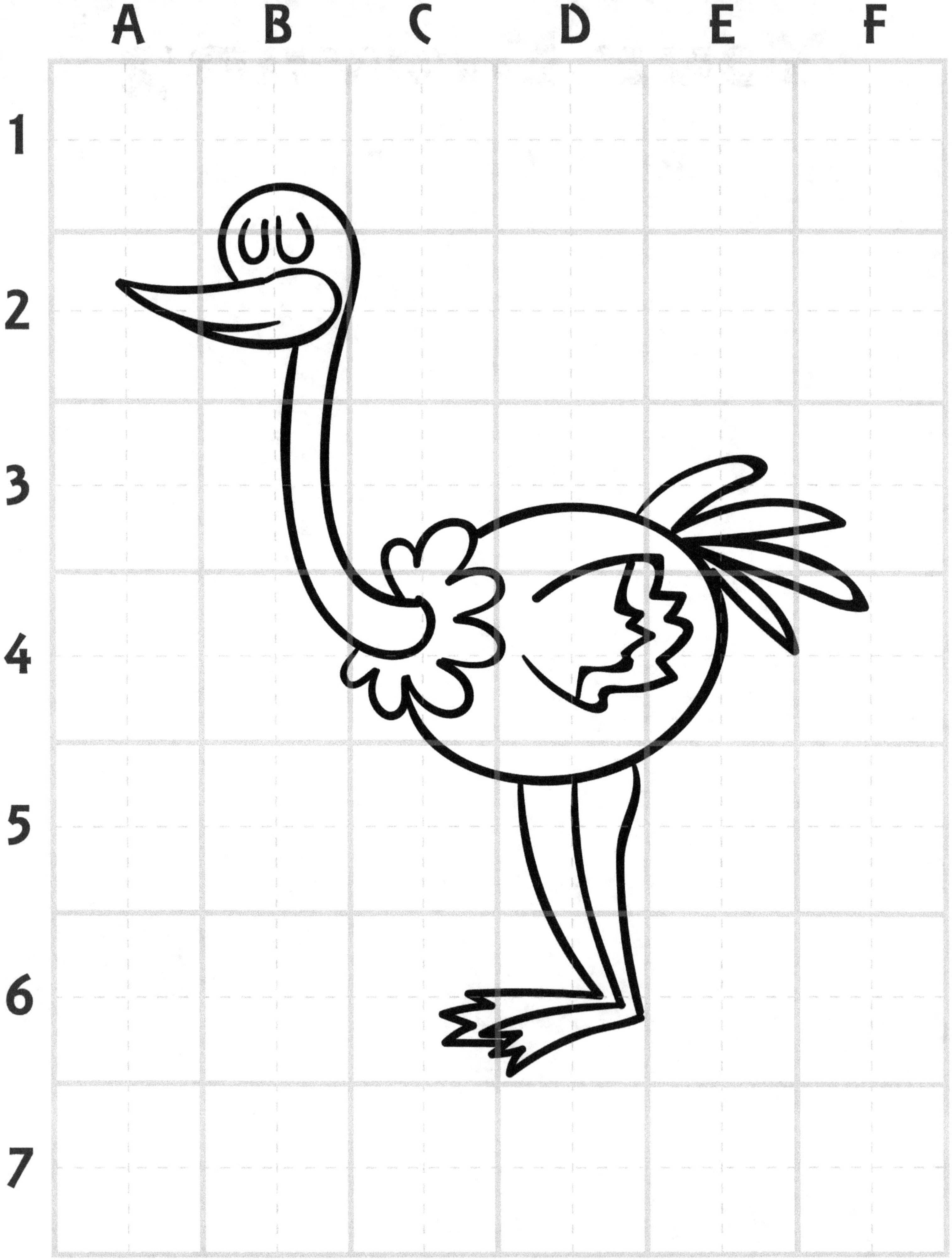
A
B
C
D
E
F
1
2
3
4
5
6
7

Your Drawing

	A	B	C	D	E	F
1						
2						
3						
4						
5						
6						
7						

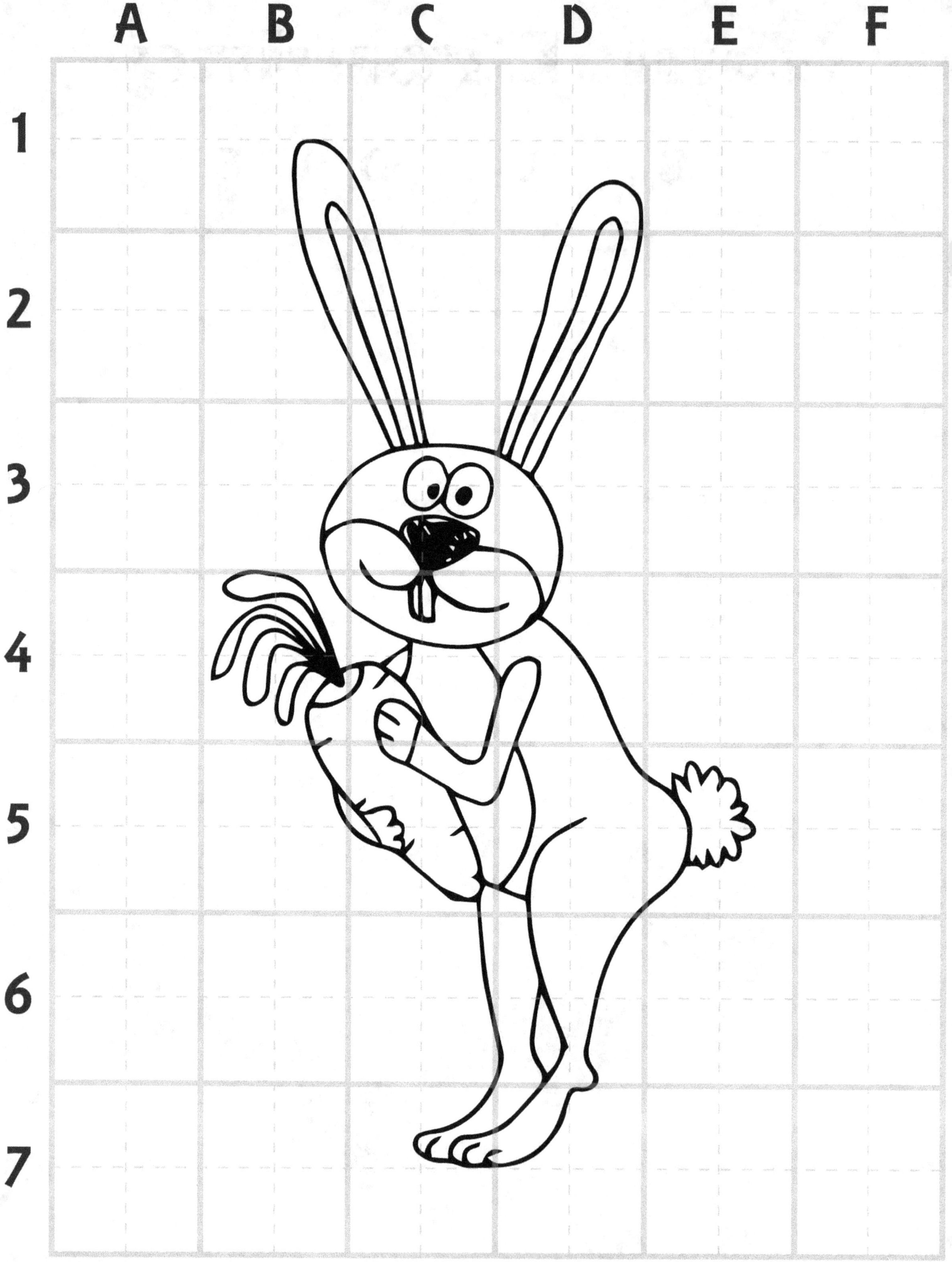
A B C D E F
1
2
3
4
5
6
7

Your Drawing

	A	B	C	D	E	F
1						
2						
3						
4						
5						
6						
7						

www.ingramcontent.com/pod-product-compliance
Lightning Source LLC
Chambersburg PA
CBHW080524220526
45465CB00006B/2587
9798748847278